MORE IRISH
COUNT

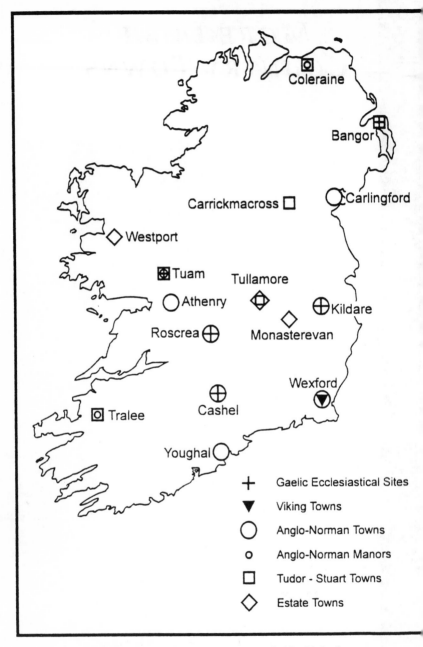

The location and origin of towns included in this book

MORE IRISH COUNTRY TOWNS

Edited by
ANNGRET SIMMS
&
J. H. ANDREWS

U.S. DISTRIBUTOR
DUFOUR EDITIONS
CHESTER SPRINGS,
PA 19425-0007
(610) 458-5005

THE THOMAS DAVIS LECTURE SERIES
General Editor: Michael Littleton

Published in association with
RADIO TELEFÍS ÉIREANN

MERCIER PRESS

MERCIER PRESS
PO Box 5, 5 French Church Street, Cork
16 Hume Street, Dublin 2

ISBN 1 85635 121 1

10 9 8 7 6 5 4 3 2 1

Acknowledgements

The editor and publisher would like to thank the trustees of the Estate of Patrick Kavanagh, c/o Peter Fallon, Literary Agent, Loughcrew, Oldcastle, Co. Meath for their kind permission to reproduce lines from 'In Memory of My Mother'; National Library of Ireland for permission to reproduce photograph of Carrickmacross Fair Day, c. 1900; The Ulster Folk and Transport Museum for permission to reproduce the photograph of Taafe's Castle, Carlingford; Cambridge University Collection of Air Photographs: copyright reserved for the aerial photograph of Tralee; Aerofilms of Borehamwood for the photograph of Monasterevan; the Ordnance Survey of Ireland for the maps based on the Ordnance Survey, by permission of the government [permit no. 6085]; and the Ordnance Survey of Northern Ireland for the maps of Coleraine and Bangor [permit no. 835], with the permission of the Controller of Her Majesty's Stationery Office.

Printed in Ireland by Colour Books Ltd.

CONTENTS

LIST OF ILLUSTRATIONS

page

LIST OF MAPS

page

PREFACE

This volume continues to tell the story of Irish country towns. Like its predecessor, it is based on a Thomas Davis lecture series, which was broadcast by Radio Telefís Éireann between June and September 1993. Mr Michael Littleton, the producer of the programme, gave great encouragement to the idea of exploring the smaller Irish towns.

These towns, despite their rather unified appearance, which they acquired in the nineteenth century, have roots in the distant past, as the general map at the beginning of this book shows us. Some of our towns, for example Cashel, Kildare, Roscrea, Tuam and Bangor have their origins in the Early Christian period, when in the tenth and eleventh centuries they were flourishing monastic sites. Our collection also includes one town, Wexford, which was founded by the Norsemen in the tenth century, as indeed Dublin, Waterford, Cork, and Limerick were. However, the largest number of Irish towns owe their origin to the Anglo-Normans, who came to Ireland in the late twelfth century. Frequently, they granted their town charters to pre-existing sites, such as the Viking town of Wexford, which was given a royal charter by Henry II, or to historic places like Kildare, Cashel or Roscrea, which we already know as the sites of important Early Christian monasteries. Another substantial group are the plantation towns. Some of these, like Bangor, were already important sites in the Early Christian period and others, like Coleraine and Tralee, have an Anglo-Norman past. The last category are the estate towns such as Westport and Monasterevan, which were attached to great estate houses. It becomes obvious from this short account how closely the origin of towns in Ireland is linked to the major phases of Irish history.

Beginning with one of our most ancient towns, Kildare, we turn to the northern part of our country and then continue south, ending in Wexford with its reminders of the Viking past. An illustration and a town plan is included with each town. The plan of Carlingford shows the beauty of the early nineteenth-century Ordnance Survey maps, engraved on copper plates. Mainly because of the larger size of the other towns, this type of map could not be used throughout. The plan of Kildare, the only town in this volume also to be produced in the *Irish Historic Towns Atlas*, illustrates the quality of the reconstruction maps for this project. As it would not be easy to recognise the historic sites mentioned in the texts on Ordnance Survey maps covering the whole of a town, Stephen Hannon and his colleague Ciaran Lynch of the Department of Geography in University College Dublin have patiently produced computer generated town plans, for which I thank them very sincerely. Once more I am most grateful to Professor John Andrews for his energetic editorial work across the Irish Sea.

I would also like to thank Bord Fáilte for its continued support of research into the Irish Heritage Towns. Also, Aer Rianta has recently adopted the theme of Irish towns. The next time you pass through Dublin airport look at the portraits of different Irish towns within the airport buildings. It is very encouraging when people from different directions come together in order to take care of a precious part of our heritage which had long been neglected for historical reasons, as Professor Andrews explains so well in his introduction to this volume.

Our small collection of town histories shows how a diversity of traditions has moulded the characteristic personalities of our towns. An awareness of this richness can be an inspiration for the townspeople of today and will contribute to the civic spirit which alone – in the long run – will sustain our towns and cities.

ANNGRET SIMMS
Department of Geography
University College Dublin

THE STUDY OF IRISH
COUNTRY TOWNS

J. H. Andrews

THE first volume of Thomas Davis lectures on Irish country towns began with a general review of urban origins and development by Professor Anngret Simms. My subject in the following paragraphs is not so much the towns themselves as how they have been studied. Let us begin with a fulsome compliment addressed to a late seventeenth-century English natural historian and topographer:

Drake and Columbus do in thee revive,
That we from thy research as much receive.
Thou art as great as they, for 'tis all one
New worlds to find or nicely to describe the known.

Finding new worlds is an ancient ambition. The impulse to throw scholarly or scientific light on one's own home district by 'nicely describing the known' was slower to make itself felt. In Ireland, for example, modern topographical literature begins only in the 1570s and early 1580s with the writings of Richard Stanihurst, though to make up for lost time these were followed in 1586 by considerable Irish coverage in William Camden's misleadingly titled *Britannia*. Towns figured prominently in this kind of publication from the outset, one reason for their popularity being that they were easier to write about than rural areas. The typical Elizabethan town was still manageably compact, and still unambiguously demarcated by an enclosing wall. It also had more to offer the descriptive writer than did the surrounding countryside, being at once richer, economically more diverse, and better endowed with buildings and monuments.

Intellectually urban history owed much of its attraction to the problem of origins. Since craftsmen, traders and clerks all have to be fed, the town must surely be a later development than the farm. Yet unlike some other human institu-

9

tions, such as the Christian church, towns could not be self-evidently ascribed to any particular founder or cradled in any particular spatio-temporal location. Their roots were thus a fitting subject for research and conjecture, the kind of conjecture that remains necessary even today in studying such ill-documented historical phenomena as the Irish monastic proto-town. A further stimulus to urban scholarship was a belief in the special virtues of civic life. Much of this interest reflected teleological presuppositions implicit in contemporary religious belief, with towns commanding approval simply as elements in the divine plan. Once pen has been put to paper, another more mundane reason for praising God's creation was the fear of offending earthly readers. Local pride, an attitude unimpressive to modern historians, was certainly treated with considerable respect by Camden, who made a point of describing most English towns as neat, fair, stately, eminent, beautified, adorned and so on. The same feeling ensured that many early urban historians were residents of the places they wrote about. An example of both the pride and its rationale in Elizabethan England was John Hooker of Exeter, for whom the very essence of townhood was a 'multitude of people assembled or collected to the end to continue and live together in a common society yielding dutiful obedience to their superiors and mutual love to [one] another'.

One wonders how many Irish writers, then or later, would have defined a town in quite the same terms as Hooker. The Gaelic view of life had long been essentially rural, with towns intruding belatedly as an alien force. The leaders of medieval Irish society copied many elements of foreign material culture, in particular castles and weaponry, but very few of them made any serious attempt to imitate the city or the borough. On the literary plane their indifference can be traced far into more peaceful times: what was the first Irish town history to be written by an author with a Gaelic-sounding name, let alone written in the Irish language?

Nor do we find much sign of civic complacency among Stanihurst's fellow Anglo-Irishmen, whether they were descendants of Norman settlers or newcomers assisting in the Tudor reconquest. These people were by no means devoid of historical curiosity, yet they would have found few grounds for satisfaction in studying the Irish middle ages. It was true that Strongbow and his colonists could be admired as a non-Roman equivalent to the Roman occupation. The Normans too had been mighty builders in the service of defence and religion, both in the obvious physical sense and as creators of a legal and administrative system, but by the sixteenth century Stanihurst could find only a handful of places worthy of approval, and there are whole counties where urban-historical writing begins with a lament. In Clare for example one reporter of 1574 enumerated half a dozen settlements of which it could be said:

> In old time these were good market towns and had English jurisdiction and were governed by portreeves and other officers by authority of the king of England, but now they are wasted and destroyed in a manner, saving the castles, and no part of the towns left but old houses of stone work, broken gates and ruinous walls.

It was not until the seventeenth century that Irish towns began to show much sign of peace and prosperity, and even then the country's historians were slow to catch up. Here Ireland differed from North America, as we can see from the literature – or lack of it – associated with the sixteenth- and seventeenth-century plantations: even in Ulster there was no writer to match William Bradford of Massachusetts or John Smith of Virginia. This Irish historiographical preference for early over recent times is shown in many published urban studies, including some in the present book. Eventually, of course, the plantations in their turn ceased to be recent, and then we find towns with a strong planter influence displaying an above-average level of self-consciousness reflected in the unusually early production of local histories. Examples are Youghal, Carrickfergus, Belfast, Birr and Bandon.

The importation of ready-made settler communities was always a localised phenomenon in early modern Ireland. In most of the country the only post-medieval planters were the new landlords, a class which whatever its other virtues was to prove something of a disappointment as a nursery for urban research. Many Irish towns, whatever their ultimate social complexion, were the creations of great landowning families, some of them active in regional and local history like Lord Walter Fitzgerald in County Kildare. But why don't Fitzgerald's writings tell how the village of Maynooth was transformed by his own ancestors? Wasn't a well-built estate town something to be proud of? The answer is that if the town was seen as an architectural adjunct to a big house and its park, then publicising it in print would probably be considered vulgar. This might explain why we find so few references to the laying out of streets and squares in even the longest and most minutely detailed books on Irish family history. If landlords had reformed the constitutions of their towns in the interest of wider self-government it might have been worth boasting about, but that is just what they did not do.

However, scholarship abhors a vacuum, and once the impulse to historical writing had appeared at the top of the urban hierarchy it would inevitably percolate to the bottom, even if not very fast. Thus Walter Harris's history of Dublin (1766) was quickly followed by John Ferrar on Limerick (1767), but there were long delays before these two pioneers were joined by Youghal (anonymous, 1784) and Carrick-fergus (Samuel McSkimin, 1811). Only after the Napoleonic wars did progress quicken with James Stuart (Armagh, 1819), James Hardiman (Galway, 1820), George Benn (Belfast, 1823), R. H. Ryland (Waterford, 1824) and others, with an understandable falling-off in the famine period before another historiographical wave began to gather strength after 1860. Even then a town as small as say Naas or Dungarvan would probably be hidden within the covers of a county history or as an article in a learned journal. Like most eighteenth- and nineteenth-century scholars the typical town historian was either a clergyman, a doctor or a lawyer – at any rate an amateur, which as everyone knows means one who works for love. For it is a well-established rule of authorship that however unpromising a writer's theme he eventually develops an affection for it, and when this happens to the chronicler of a town he is unlikely to spend much time on features that were common to a great many other places. On the contrary, most of his space will be dedicated to local 'worthies' – not only eminent individuals, but also whatever buildings, monuments and institutions convey a sense of rarity or even uniqueness. He will also search the pages of national history in quest of great events for which his town has briefly and fortuitously provided the stage. In due course this feeling for local particularity may inspire a more generalised approach to the study of towns. Among the older historians, however, there is seldom any impression of the urban community as a whole. It is a failure matched in iconographical terms by the remarkable shortage of pre-twentieth-century Irish pictures showing neighbour-hoods or streets, let alone complete townscapes, as opposed to individual buildings.

Particularity was also cultivated by the many tourists who developed the journal-writing habit in the eighteenth and nineteenth centuries, among the earliest and most observant of these being Richard Pococke, Arthur Young, Daniel Augustus Beaufort and Coquebert de Montbret. The traveller's motives and capacities differed from those of sedentary historians. He had no time for minute research or reasoned generalisation; on the other hand he could afford to ignore local opinion, especially if his record was intended only for family and friends or perhaps for posterity. Beaufort for instance in 1787-8 was far from easily pleased; but at least when he called Castlebar extremely well-built, and Lisburn a prodigious pretty town, we can be sure that he meant what he said.

On the foregoing interpretation it is no surprise that the first comparative and synthetic accounts of Irish towns should be conceived in a critical rather than an adulatory spirit. In Britain such studies were inspired by a growing disharmony between ancient local-government structures and the new facts of industrial life, especially where mush-rooming communities like nineteenth-century Manchester remained frozen into the administrative status of a mere village. In Ireland this kind of runaway growth was less

13

spectacular: here the more obvious anomalies were the 'rotten boroughs', miniscule in size and wealth but for obscure historical reasons still technically urban. When the government took a survey of contemporary Irish municipal corporations in 1835-6 its findings were almost uniformly censorious. To quote at random:

> In many towns there is no recognised commonalty ... in others, where existing in name, it is entirely disproportioned to the inhabitants and consists of a small portion of an exclusive character, not comprising the mercantile interests, nor representing the wealth, intelligence or respectability of the town. The corporation are, not without reason, looked on by the great body of the inhabitants of the corporate districts with suspicion and distrust, as having interests distinct from and adverse to those of the general community, who they thus studiously exclude from a participation in the municipal government.

One result of the mid- and late- nineteenth-century urge for improvement was the collection and publication of socio-economic data at government expense, often in the form of statistics and maps. In earlier social and geographical surveys, it had been rare for towns to dictate their own scale of treatment (John Speed's atlas of 1612 was a notable exception), much more common to squeeze them uncomfortably within the framework of a county or parish. From the 1830s all this was changed by both official and private publishers. The coverage of towns in Samuel Lewis's *Topographical Dictionary of Ireland* (1837), for instance, is probably the best feature of that magnificent book. In the new population censuses and in the Ordnance Survey, a town was defined simply by its size: thus the census recognised two urban grades – more than 20 houses made a 'town', more than 2,000 people qualified as a 'civic district' with a larger quota of published information. The Ordnance Survey drew many colourful town plans on enlarged scales, the criterion finally adopted for publishing these being a population of 4,000. Even in Ireland such generous limits drew in an impressively large number of specimens, most of them looking very much alike when viewed through a statistical or cartographic lens. Yet little of this information was properly digested by contemporary experts, for the simple reason that small-town problems seemed less serious than those of either rural small-holdings or big-city slums. It was only in retrospect that twentieth-century academics finally began to adjust the balance, and by that time much of the unpublished census material had been lost (it survives best for 1901 and 1911) and much of the map evidence forgotten. Meanwhile an important exception to the rule of nineteenth-century inaction had been the gradual reform of local government by widening the franchise, remodelling the tax-base, investing municipal authorities with powers appropriate to contemporary life, and rationalising the boundaries of urban areas. These changes too made Irish towns seem more alike, but at least their administration had ceased to be a matter of scandal and concern.

It is the vast expansion of third-level education in our own age that has done more than anything else to change the face of Irish urban studies, as will be evident from the number of chapters in the book and its predecessor that have been written by university lecturers. These newcomers to the urban scene could choose from two traditions: on the one hand the local dedication of the nineteenth-century historian, on the other the neutrality of the civil servant. Both ideals are well exemplified in geography, which is the discipline best represented in the following pages. On the one hand town life could be treated as an abstraction, in the hope that scientific methods would bring each particular case under some overriding general rule. In early twentieth-century geography books, the main requirement for a successful town was the 'nodality' created by a convergence of routes, as at a pass, gap, ford, bridge, or head of navigation. Given this notion of each town as a point on a small-scale map, its geographical significance would be as a centre of collection and distribution and its status could be gauged from the number and extent of its 'hinterlands', which would in turn depend on its nodality. Irish hinterland studies had been pioneered by the government in the 1830s with the use of recent maps and surveys to create town-centred poor law unions, later converted into administrative rural districts. In the Irish Free State they received further official recognition

15

when the North-eastern Boundary Bureau drew maps showing how the new border of 1921 had separated a number of towns from their traditional spheres of influence. Among academic geographers the same idea bore fruit nearly thirty years later when Professor J. P. Haughton traced the circulation areas of Irish local newspapers, and again when a number of more detailed hinterland surveys were conducted by scholars of the next generation.

Geographical influence works in different ways at different periods. In the modern age a river crossing may attract more people, in earlier times a hill top. Awareness of such differences has brought an interest in town-typology as a happy medium between the individual and the universal, and one particularly fruitful basis of classification has been the historical origins of our towns. Examples can be found in two notable geographical publications: by T. W. Freeman in his book, *Ireland* (1950) and by Anngret Simms in the *Atlas of Ireland* (1979) edited by J. P. Haughton for the Royal Irish Academy. Each of these geographers, it should be noted, acknowledged the co-operation of an historical colleague, and much subsequent writing on settlement evolution – including the present book – has been the product of co-operative work by both disciplines.

Such classifications still treat each town as a single point. But any settlement in which thousands of square metres are occupied by hundreds of people must also be seen as a collection of parts. Who lives in a town, where do they come from, which neighbourhoods do they occupy, how do they interact, what is their source of income and is it good enough to deter them from emigrating? Between the 1940s and 1960s Irish geographers made many illuminating studies of individual small towns as viewed from the inside, most of them under the direction of two scholars already mentioned – Walter Freeman and Joe Haughton. These researchers illustrate the second, regional tradition of modern geography, akin in some ways to early topographical writing but with partisanship left aside and with social groups replacing the selected 'worthies' of an earlier age. From the way the behavioural sciences developed after 1970 one might have expected this descriptive approach to be refined by a more overtly statistical processing of questionnaires and interviews. On the whole this did not happen, and in the 1980s an eminent geographer was still deploring our ignorance of the social geography of Ireland's smaller population centres. More than ten years later, no professional sociologist has come forward in this book to say whether the notorious problems of inner cities have been spreading to country towns. Shortage of academic manpower can no longer be pleaded as an excuse for this neglect, but one long-standing inhibition may still remain effective. Small towns are a small world, in which there is more than a sporting chance that the victims of a sociologist's published case-study might recognise their neighbours and themselves. It may be no accident that so much grass-roots sociology has been the work of foreigners: when Irishmen anatomise their neighbours it is more often through the medium of novels and plays.

In these circumstances we need not be surprised or disappointed to see scholars turning from the social to the physical dimension: if we can't save a town's soul we can at least do something for its body. And in Ireland it was no doubt predictable that these 'morphological' studies too would in due course come to be heavily influenced by the past. The historical significance of urban form was urged on English-speaking readers as long ago as 1933:

> The vestiges of urban growth are not the documentary sources of ordinary historical research. Rather they are the remains of walls, gates and buildings, traces of ditch and embankment, lines of streets, market places and parish boundaries.

These are the words of an American scholar, Carl Stephenson. (A few paragraphs later he made good his only obvious omission by also recommending place names as a source of evidence.) At the time and for long afterwards, British and Irish historians paid little attention to this inspiring message, despite the wealth of large-scale map evidence at their disposal. It is true that many geographers of Stephenson's generation were interested in spatial patterns, but they made a false start by trying to classify the layouts of entire towns, a process that soon yielded almost as many classes as there were individuals. In Ireland Walter Freeman went to the other extreme by reducing the number of types to one, but signalled the half-seriousness of this solution when he christened his ideal specimen with the not very amusing name of Ballydull, 'built by the earl of Slowtown'. At least this was to recognise that history had called the tune: the straight lines and right angles of the streets in Freeman's map of 'Ballydull' were unmistakably characteristic of a pre-famine estate town. But even the most archetypical landlord towns may be open to a 'gradualist' interpretation, as Arnold Horner has shown by reconstructing the pre-estate topography of Maynooth and Monasterevan. When, as so often happens, a town evolves by slow degrees, much of its growth may date from periods beyond the reach of surviving documentary, cartographic or architectural evidence: then the historian must draw on his analogical powers to 'read' the layout of streets and boundaries by deciding which of any two lines is likely to be older than the other. In the jargon of those who enjoy jargon we thus move from morphology to morphogenesis, classifying not complete towns but the ways in which a town may grow.

Various influences have encouraged a morphogenetic approach among the present generation of urban historians in a number of countries. One is the accelerating pace of building and rebuilding. Some of this was due to aerial bombardment in Second World War; and many towns that escaped bombing were subsequently redeveloped to accommodate a huge increase in car ownership. Site clearance may allow at least a brief opportunity for archaeological excavation: in this respect Ireland's small towns have been unlucky, though some archaeologists have tried to fill the gap with imaginative re-interpretations of non-archaeological evidence. Another factor of some historiographical importance has been the unpopularity of modern architecture, so that nineteenth- and early twentieth-century buildings and townscapes once despised now began to look almost beautiful by comparison and certainly worth preserving for use and study. Given this mixture of motives, a medieval street might have a good chance of revival as a pedestrian precinct.

All in all, the most promising influence on the study of urban form in recent years has been an alliance of two previously unrelated interests: on the one hand the scholarly researcher, on the other the public or private institution with money to spend. In the Republic of Ireland this affinity has been signalled in the 1980s and 1990s by a network of mutually beneficial relationships involving Bord Failte's Heritage Town programme, the Urban Archaeology Survey directed by John Bradley, and the Royal Irish Academy's *Atlas of Irish Historic Towns* now being edited by Anngret Simms, Howard Clarke and Raymond Gillespie. Such efforts deserve to be more widely known and supported. In the last resort, however, everything must depend on individual scholars like those who have contributed to this book.

Select bibliography
T. W. Freeman, 'The Irish country town,' *Irish Geography*, iii (1954), pp. 5-14
L. M. Cullen: *Irish Towns and Villages*, Dublin, 1979
D. G. Pringle: 'The Irish urban system, an overview', *Geographical Viewpoint*, ix (1980), pp. 29-48
D. Harkness and M. O'Dowd (eds): *The Town in Ireland*, Belfast, 1981
H. B. Clarke and A. Simms (eds), *The Comparative History of Urban Origins in Non-Roman Europe: Ireland, Wales, Denmark, Germany, Poland and Russia from the Ninth to the Thirteenth Century*, BAR International Series, 255, i and ii, Oxford, 1985
Irish Historic Towns Atlas: Editors J. H. Andrews, A. Simms, H. B. Clarke, R. Gillespie, no. 1 *Kildare* by J. H. Andrews (1986), no. 2 *Carrickfergus* by P. Robinson (1986), no. 3 *Bandon* by P. O'Flanagan (1988), no. 4 *Kells* by A. Simms with K. Simms (1990), no. 5 *Mullingar* by J. H. Andrews with K. M. Davies (1992), no. 6 *Athlone* by H. Murtagh (1994), no. 7 *Maynooth* by A. A. Horner (1995), no. 8 *Downpatrick* by R. H. Buchanan and A. Wilson (1996), Royal Irish Academy, Dublin

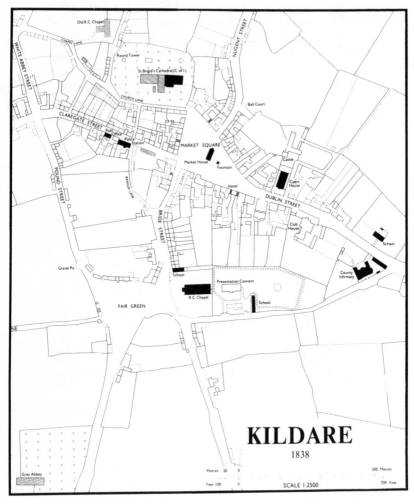

Kildare 1838, Irish Historic Towns Atlas, 1986

KILDARE

J. H. Andrews

THIS book, like so much speaking and writing in Ireland, is mainly concerned with various aspects of the past, so perhaps it is appropriate to begin this chapter with one of the earliest events in the history of human culture. Since people learnt to use fire before they learned to make fire, there must have been a time when in every community at least one flame – to contemporaries, probably a sacred flame – could never be allowed to go out. And in religious observances this custom might conceivably have been preserved, through age after age of pagan worship, until the advent of Christianity and even beyond. The example I have in mind is the perpetual fire watched over by a famous community of Irish nuns. Their founder, St Brigid, lived six centuries after Christ, and six centuries after St Brigid her fire was still alight. And in her town of Kildare 'Firehouse' and 'Fire Castle' remain on record as traditional placenames even in our own time. Had Brigid's fire been originally fuelled by heathens? Does her saint's day in February mark an earlier pagan festival? Had she herself begun her career as a pagan priestess? Did she also inherit a pre-Christian holy tree, the very tree perhaps that is commemorated in the place name *Cill Dara*, 'the church of the oak'?

Many of Ireland's pagan shrines were located where they could be easily seen from a considerable distance. The same is true of many of our earliest monasteries. Sometimes we find a pair of anciently settled hills in close proximity, one heathen and one Christian, like Knockaulin and Old Kilcullen in County Kildare, or like Tara and Skreen in County Meath. Brigid could have celebrated her conversion, if she had wanted to, by moving to Silliott Hill a mile and a half south-west of Kildare Hill, but if she was herself a pre-Christian she would have felt no danger of spiritual contamination from pre-Christian influences. The traditions of a

Kildare from the north in c. 1794 by William Beauford
(Anthologia Hibernica)

perpetual fire that I mentioned a moment ago all relate to the crest of the ridge now occupied by the town of Kildare, close to the round tower built by Brigid's successors. The doors of these towers, we are told, opened to face the principal church of a monastic settlement, which suggests that although nothing survives of Brigid's wooden church its site is almost certainly marked by the massive cathedral now dedicated to her. The round tower happily survives, crowning the horizon as seen from all the numerous country roads that still converge upon Kildare. On some of these roads one can even now imagine oneself an early Christian pilgrim, heartened by the prospect of his journey's end. And looking outwards from the churchyard one can easily remember an old biographer's description of St Brigid, praising the glories of earth and sky as she watched the sun rise over the Wicklow Mountains with the flowers and trees glittering in the morning light.

All of which is said in deference to those scholars who make the antiquity of Irish civilisation a matter of national pride. On a more narrow-minded view, the urban historian's responsibility begins not at the dawn of human history but only when he and his contemporaries would recognise a town. When *would* we recognise a town in Kildare, or anywhere else for that matter? Even after fifteen Thomas Davis lectures this remains a difficult question, but part of the answer can be given with some confidence. A town is more than a single institution. It is more than a barracks or hospital or airport, more than a monastery or nunnery, however much ground these places may occupy, however many people may work in them, and however many different functions they may discharge. St Brigid's nunnery, which later doubled as a monastery, became a centre for education, art and even politics as well as for worship, but for our present argument these other activities are beside the point. What does matter is that any large institution can attract its own camp followers, a term I use with no derogatory overtones, and these by a kind of multiplier-effect can exercise a similar magnetic force. When the resulting process of accretion has gone far enough we may indeed begin to speak of a town, though we are unlikely to do so until the settlement in question consists mainly of independent residential units, inhabited by people who do not all work for the same employer. In a town, people must co-operate without being under orders to do so, which explains why they so often fail to co-operate.

But this still leaves us with the problem of differentiating towns from villages. Various criteria for urban identity have been suggested, but in a historical context these are often either unacceptable or inapplicable. For instance, scholarly opinion in several countries has now turned against defining towns as chartered boroughs or other purely constitutional entities; and for the antiquity-loving scholars I mentioned earlier this is just as well, because on a constitutional definition pre-Norman Ireland was 100 per cent rural. For most historians, it is economic life that makes a town, and in Ireland our early evidence of economic life is to say the least fragmentary. In tenth-century Kildare we know that the king of Leinster's horse took fright at a pair of antlers intended to be made into combs. But one craftsman or one workshop can hardly serve to classify a whole community: nobody would postulate a town in Victorian Ireland wherever a blacksmith had his forge. Or take a second piece of evidence. In twelfth-century Kildare we know that coins were dropped or buried on the site of the round tower. But had their owner ever bought or sold anything in Kildare itself or even anywhere near it? Those combs and coins are not just chosen as striking examples. They are our *only* examples of economic life from half a millennium of Kildare history.

Authorities on other towns have confronted this dearth of evidence in their own way. In this case for once we can do more than sift through the fragments. A seventh-century writer anticipated our question and left us a direct answer. His name was Cogitosus and he earns our respect by acknowledging implicitly that towns and even cities are difficult to define. As a user of the Latin language, Cogitosus's concept of a city was no doubt ultimately derived from Roman sources. Anyway it is a word that he had little hesitation in applying to Kildare, not once but four times. No other town in Ireland, not even Armagh, can produce so definite an endorsement from such an early date. Of course we don't have to believe everything an old writer chooses to tell us, but Cogitosus had a serious purpose – writing the life of St Brigid, no less – and there were surely limits to the amount of exaggeration that his contemporaries would let him get away with.

But whatever urban qualities Cogitosus may have found in Kildare, one quality that it seems to have lacked is an urban shape. Many of Ireland's early ecclesiastical settlements were surrounded by circular or oval banks and ditches, some of which can still be seen on the ground while others have clearly influenced the course of modern roads, fences and property boundaries. There are some traces of such a circular alignment in Kildare, most notably the street in the north-west of the town now known as Priest's Lane. These enclosures were intended not for defence against physical force but rather to draw a line between sacred and profane. The exact shape of the consecrated area has been explained as an image or microcosm of God's whole creation, and one historian, seeking a wider context for our problem, points out that the Latin word *urbs*, a city, derives from the same linguistic source as the word 'orb', a sphere or globe. Against this, we have to admit that most towns known to have been inhabited by Latin-speakers outside Ireland were far from circular in shape. Here as in other respects the Roman and the modern town are much alike, both being shaped by economic forces and particularly by competition for access. It is this competition that gives a typical modern house-plot the form of a narrow rectangle with its short side fronting the public highway. No assemblage of such rectangles will add up to a circular outline. But at this point I leave the discussion of urban shapes hanging awkwardly in mid-air, if only because it would be wrong to suggest that every problem of Irish urban history has been solved. Let us just take note that here is one difference between a town as we conceive it and Kildare as created by St Brigid, because most historians would agree that the people who created rectangular towns in Ireland didn't arrive until the twelfth century.

The Normans are best known in this country as soldiers, administrators and builders but one of them was an author. Giraldus Cambrensis was writing some fifteen years after the Anglo-Norman conquest of Leinster and he described the conquered territory in much the same terms that Julius Caesar had applied to Britain 1,200 years earlier. Both writers are unmistakably clear about the absence of towns in the Celtic world. Had Cogitosus been mistaken after all? Or was Giraldus mistaken? Or had the country they were describing changed in the meantime? There was at least one thread of continuity between them. Giraldus spent several pages on the various legends associated with Kildare, including the pastures that renewed themselves overnight no matter how intensively they were grazed (presumably a reference to what is now called the Curragh), the fire that left no ashes, the falcon that lived for 600 years, and the book dictated by an angel. Kildare may have declined since Cogitosus's time, but at least Giraldus knew that every one of these marvels was in some way connected with its founding saint. Which makes it seem safe to say that without Brigid there would be no modern town here.

Apart from the church, the only building that Giraldus

mentions in twelfth-century Kildare is one that nuns and monks would never have considered necessary, a castle recently built by the Norman lord of Leinster. It is common enough for colonial invaders to choose pre-existing habitations for development, but many Irish monastic sites were too inaccessible, or too unpromising economically, to be adopted as towns by the Normans. No one would describe the ridge at Kildare as inaccessible; in fact the average motorist probably isn't even aware of climbing it; and in the surrounding plain of Kildare, as Giraldus called it, a small town could procure quite enough food to support itself. The ease of communications to Brigid's church had already been recognised in pre-Norman times by making Kildare the seat of a bishop. By the early fourteenth century the Normans had made it a parish, a manor, and a borough, as well as applying its name to a shire and then to an earldom. The earls of Kildare and their descendants remained the principal landowners in the town until the twentieth century, with the church taking second place until it was disestablished in Queen Victoria's time.

The ridge of Kildare has two distinct summits, again barely noticeable to the casual observer but still quite distinct and separated by a saddle of slightly lower ground underlying the present market place. The north-western of the two summits was occupied by the cathedral and round tower. The south-east summit carries a square tower, obviously medieval, but according to the architectural experts not one of the late-medieval fortified dwellings familiar in many Irish main streets. In fact the non-expert can work this out for himself, because unlike most of our town castles this one is behind the other houses. It stands well back from the street beside a polygonal open space which was once a bawn or bailey comparable in size with those of other high-ranking medieval fortresses like Athlone, Kilkenny and Limerick. Although all but one of its four towers have long since disappeared, the defensive qualities of this site are still evident from the steep drop that separates the original castle from the modern houses and gardens outside. The Ordnance Survey optimistically describes the bawn as a park but at present it looks more like some kind of junk yard.

Medieval Kildare was thus dominated by two compact enclosures, one ecclesiastical and one secular. St Brigid's monastery continued to lose power and prestige during this period – at one stage the archbishop of Dublin ordered its fire to be put out – and it seems to have been less prosperous and less influential than the Franciscan and Carmelite friaries founded by the Anglo-Normans on the outskirts of the town. It certainly failed to maintain its topographical influence on the surrounding settlement, and this makes it hard to distinguish the Early Christian from the Anglo-Norman contributions to the layout of the present streets. Unfortunately the earliest large-scale map of Kildare dates only from the mid-eighteenth century and that shows the town centre much as it is now, with a more or less straight main street along the southern, more gently sloping flank of the ridge, and with numerous long and narrow rectangular house plots. It seems plausible to attribute these features to Anglo-Norman planning, and some of the street edges are straight enough to have been set out by a surveyor. Less easily categorised is the market square, actually not square but triangular. The base of the triangle is part of the main street. Its apex, and its highest point, and its most north-westerly point, is the entrance to the cathedral churchyard. A north-west – south-east relation between churchyard and market place is common to many Irish towns that started life as early monasteries, too common to have originated by chance. It commemorates an economy in which the church and the adjacent buildings still provided most of the market trader's customers.

The number of householders with borough privileges in early fourteenth-century Kildare has been estimated by one scholar as 945, most of them probably Englishmen. This may well have represented the town's maximum pre-twentieth-century size. At any rate it is not likely to have grown very much in late medieval times. The earl, it is true, had now become the most powerful man in Ireland, but as a place to live in he preferred Maynooth, perhaps because it was more accessible from Dublin. In any case being the most powerful

27

man doesn't necessarily count for much in a state of political disintegration and civil strife. In such anarchic conditions Kildare was less favourably located than it had seemed to Giraldus Cambrensis. Unconquered midland bogs and forest were ominously close at hand, and when the English Pale was defined at the end of the fifteenth century Kildare was left outside the protected area. It was at about this time that the town was first authorised to surround itself with a wall. Some kind of enclosure was actually built, as the present-day name Claregate Street may still attest, but the wall can hardly have been very substantial because today its course is almost impossible to trace on the ground or on the map. At any rate it did not save Kildare from being described as quite empty after an Irish attack in the year 1600.

The troubles of the fifteenth and sixteenth centuries left several permanent legacies in this part of Ireland. One was the transfer of county administration from Kildare to Naas, in other words from outside to inside the English Pale. Another, following Henry VIII's attempted Protestant reformation, was an urban community almost wholly alienated from what was left of the local cathedral. Catholics eventually built their own churches in the town, one with a spire that dwarfs every other building in sight. But they never made Kildare a Catholic diocesan capital. That privilege was reserved for Carlow, which by the time it was chosen had five times as many people as Kildare.

One other change of geographical circumstance remains to be mentioned. Most of the towns that have flourished in medieval and modern Ireland are on rivers, preferably navigable rivers but if unnavigable then still useful for domestic, industrial and sanitary purposes. The only two important rivers in the area immediately west of Dublin are the Liffey and the Barrow, and Kildare stands beside neither of these; in fact it lies about halfway between them. Nor was this disability ever to be remedied by building a canal, as happened at so many of the surrounding towns. One of St Brigid's many miracles was to quench the thirst of seventeen church congregations from a single barrel for days on end, but this particular achievement was not repeated, and even

28

domestic water was far from plentiful on the Kildare ridge, while except for a few short-lived windmills there was no natural source of inanimate energy. The lack of industry in Irish towns is now recognised as a historical myth, disproved not far away by the great distillery at Monasterevan, the Osbertown Mills near Naas, and the woollen factories at Celbridge and Ballymore Eustace. At Kildare the myth is true and one important source of eighteenth- and nineteenth-century income and employment was unavailable. When the town was investigated by a government commission on municipal boroughs in 1835 its population was found to be less than 2,000. Not surprisingly, the commission recommended that Kildare should cease to be a borough. Not surprisingly, the recommendation was accepted.

The best that this newly demoted village could offer was to be on the way to somewhere more interesting. At one stage even that was asking too much. In the seventeenth century all the converging pilgrim routes I mentioned earlier had been implicitly classified as lanes by an author who described Kildare as 'not lying in any road'. But at least it lay in a straight line from Dublin to Limerick and as long-distance traffic began to flourish in the following century its main street became part of a turnpike road between these two cities, carrying goods and passengers to and from a number of newly flourishing midland towns. A century later the railways gave Kildare station command of the main routes not just to Limerick but also to Cork and Waterford. Of course a railway has little power to generate passing trade, and in this case its only visible legacies were a handsome station-house, some railway workers' cottages, and a hotel which no one bothered to rebuild after it was burnt down a few years ago. A more lasting achievement of the railways was to set a precedent for the enormously increased road traffic of our own century. Kildare now found itself on the main motor road from Dublin to Cork and in the 1980s it may well have been the smallest town in Ireland with its own set of traffic lights.

But why should any motorist stop longer than it takes for the lights to change? One answer takes us back to St

Brigid's request for as much land as she could cover with her cloak. The Curragh of Kildare has been noted since the seventeenth century for riding, hawking, hunting, racing and war-games, activities later given permanent expression in a race course and a military barracks. In the 1890s the nearby town began to grow in sympathy and a few army officers and equestrian enthusiasts struck a faintly exotic note by building late-Victorian or Edwardian style houses in the surrounding area at a time when most of rural Ireland was still sleeping through its long post-Georgian twilight. Members of the same social group no doubt also encouraged the restoration of the Church of Ireland cathedral at this time. Today Kildare's distinctive character owes much to this curious mixture of ecclesiastical, military and sporting influences, though the prevailing atmosphere is that of a typical Irish country town. But does it look the part of an historic town?

Remembering Professor Anngret Simms's exhortations in the first essay of this series (printed in *Irish Country Towns*, 1994) it may be salutary to remind ourselves of what has been lost: most of the earl's castle, all the dean and chapter's castle, the bishop's palace, a complete thirteenth-century abbey, the town wall except for one possible fragment in the so-called park, three gate-houses, the seventeenth-century tholsel or town hall, the lodge where Lord Edward Fitzgerald once lived, the Kildare Coffee House, later known as the Turf Club, the Deanery, the Railway Hotel, the original catholic chapel and every thatched house except one. Those are the losses, most of them suffered in what by Irish standards have been comparatively peaceful times. Fortunately the list of historic survivals is also impressive. Some of them I have already mentioned. Others include a part of the medieval Grey Abbey, a fine eighteenth-century town house, a restored market building of the same period, the slightly later county infirmary, subsequently rebuilt as a hotel, and from the early nineteenth century the courthouse, St Brigid's Catholic church, the Presentation convent, two small schools, and of course a large number of dwelling houses, although 'of course' is a phrase we should also stop using if we wish to preserve our historic past. Kildare readers may be left to finish this survey for themselves. But in making such lists we must always remember how much a town may owe not just to its individual buildings but to the arrangement of these buildings and of the streets that connect them. Perhaps it is in its juxtapositions that Kildare does most to inspire historical awareness. To stand between cathedral precinct and market place, between religious and secular domains, is to command one of the most thought-provoking panoramas that the Irish landscape has to offer.

Select bibilography
'Ancient and present state of the borough of Kildare', *Anthologia Hibernica*, iii (1794), pp. 239-42
W. Fitzgerald: 'The castle of Kildare', *Journal of the County Kildare Archaeological Society*, iii (1902), pp. 486-8
M. Craig and W. Garner: *Buildings of Architectural and Historical Interest in Co. Kildare*, Dublin, 1973
A. Horner: 'New maps of Co. Kildare interest in the National Library of Ireland', *Journal of the County Kildare Archaeological Society*, xv (1975-6), pp. 473-89
T. Hayden: *St Brigid and Kildare Cathedral*, Naas, 1979
J. H. Andrews: 'Kildare', *Irish Historic Towns Atlas*, no. 1, Dublin, 1986

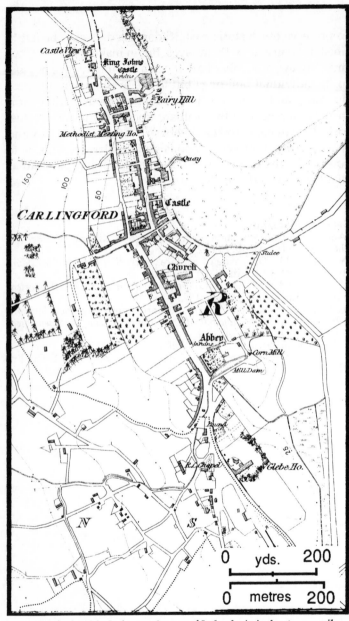

Carlingford 1836, Ordnance Survey of Ireland, six inches to one mile

CARLINGFORD

Carol Gleeson

CARLINGFORD is in the Republic of Ireland, in the north-east corner of County Louth, six miles from the border of Northern Ireland. It is situated on the southern shores of Carlingford Lough, a glacially formed inlet and one of the most beautiful sea loughs on the coast of Ireland. The lough is flanked by the Mountains of Mourne to the north and the Carlingford mountain range to the south. The foothills of the Carlingford mountains merge with a flat, fertile peninsula which stretches like a piece of patchwork towards the Irish Sea. This is the legendary Cooley peninsula, scene of Cuchulainn's defence of Ulster against the armies of Maeve of Connacht recounted in the ancient saga of the Táin Bo Cuailgne. Carlingford has a population of approximately 650 and it covers an area of roughly two square miles. Dundalk, the county capital, is located 14 miles to the south-west and Newry, in County Down, lies ten miles to the north. The main Dublin-Belfast road connects Dundalk and Newry, avoiding the peninsula, and one has to take a circuitous route to reach the tiny town of Carlingford.

The peninsula has been borderland throughout the history of the country, bounding an extensive drumlin belt which physically divides the Ulster and Leinster regions. The area contained one of the few passes through this geographical barrier, a place called The Gap of the North or the Moyry Pass. The distribution of archaeological monuments shows contrasting patterns between the northern and southern parts of the island and our ancient Irish literature corroborates the physical evidence of the very theme of the Táin Bo Cuailgne. The physical and cultural border in this region was reinforced through the structure of the early medieval Gaelic lordships and provinces, the Anglo-Norman marchlands and the seventeenth-century plantation of Ulster. The history of the peninsula reflects these influences, which are

Taaffe's Castle, Carlingford (Ulster Folk and Transport Museum)

manifested in the strong cultural identity with the legend of
the Táin, the history of colonisation and settlement in
Cooley, and the origins and development of the frontier
town of Carlingford.

There is yet another element to the history of this place,
one that did not exert much influence yet left an indelible
mark. The Vikings sailed up the lough in the ninth century
and called it Cairlinn Fjord, or 'the ford of the old woman' in
Norse. They would have noticed a small natural harbour on
the southern shore, sheltered by a rocky promontory to the
north and by Slieve Foy to the west. The harbour had probably attracted a scatter of fishermen's huts, the successors of
a tradition of use from mesolithic times when a wandering
band of hunters left tell-tale middens on the shore. Where
exactly the Viking bases were on the lough we do not know
but they would have found it hard to resist the hospitality of

this place.

However, it is only from Anglo-Norman times that we have real evidence of occupation in Carlingford. The first documentary reference dates to 1184 when John de Courcy granted the revenue of the Carlingford ferry to the abbot of Downpatrick. King John, lord of Ireland, granted the lands of Cooley and north Louth to the de Verdon family between 1189 and 1191. The eastern part of Cooley was given to Hugh de Lacy by this family in 1195 as part of a marriage settlement. The Normans realised how much potential the place had when they chose it as a defensive point on the lough and on the northern border of their territory. The castles of Carlingford and Greencastle, built fifty years later at the foot of the Mournes, gave the Normans control of the mouth of the lough. King John's castle was at least partially constructed when the king himself visited it in 1210. It was built on the promontory which overlooks the harbour and beneath its protective shadow the medieval town of Carlingford developed.

Imagine the town laid out on a map, a long narrow settlement on a north-south axis, curving slightly around the harbour which bounds the town to the east and running along the foot of Slieve Foy, within the girdle of the medieval town wall, to the west. The town is delimited by the Norman castle to the north and the modern Catholic church to the south. The layout adheres in principle to the original Norman pattern which consisted of two parallel streets running from north to south and linked by the market square which subdivides the two streets into four, Tholsel Street leading into Newry Street and Dundalk Street leading onto the Back Lane. Dwelling plots, known as burgage plots, were laid out on either side of the streets, the boundaries of which have not changed much in the intervening centuries. The town is full of little lanes which connect the streets to each other, the harbour and the town wall.

Let us embark on a brief tour of the most prominent features of this medieval town, beginning with the castle, the first fortified stone structure to be constructed in Carlingford. The building occurred in three phases. The western courtyard was built in the early thirteenth century and in the mid thirteenth century the living quarters and great hall were built to the east. The south-east portion of the castle was renovated in the late fifteenth or early sixteenth century. Despite this fortification the town was not immune to attack and there are a number of references to raids by the native Irish and Scots. These incidents would have influenced the authorities to pass a law in 1495 enacting that none but Englishmen should henceforth be constables. By 1549 the castle was described as being in 'a wretched condition'.

From the castle we walk across the railway bridge, constructed in the 1870s, to the point where Newry Street and the Back Lane converge. Travel down the Back Lane towards the Square. Look to your right and you will glimpse the fragment of the old town wall bounding the elongated back gardens of the houses that front onto the street. The first references to the establishment of town defences were in 1326 when a charter was introduced allowing for the implementation of a mural or wall tax. Only a small part of the original wall survives but it is possible to trace its route along a modern field boundary which occupies its place today. A number of musket loops date this portion of the wall to the fifteenth or sixteenth century. Town walls not only functioned as a means of defence but also acted as a definite line of demarcation between the townspeople and their rural neighbours, between Norman and Gael, and as a customs barrier to ensure that goods entering the town from the surrounding hinterland did so via the town gates where taxes were levied.

The Market Square was positioned at the heart of the old town, within a few hundred yards of the harbour and the town gates. In 1227 Hugh de Lacy received a grant from the king to hold an annual fair from 25 to 28 August. In 1358 Lionel, earl of Ulster, received permission to hold a market every Tuesday and Queen Elizabeth changed the market day to Saturday. The square does not possess a market cross but it has a number of medieval fragments attesting its antiquity, a stone head on a butcher's shop front, a blocked-up medieval window in the cellar of the pharmacy, and up until a few years ago a fine example of a medieval chimney near the doctor's house. The site of one of the town gates, the Spout Gate, lay half way up the lane which leads westwards towards the mountain. A stream once ran from the Spout Gate over the square to the harbour and supplied fresh water for the townspeople. Nothing now remains of this gate but it was still in existence when Isaac Butler visited the town in 1744.

Let us leave the square and continue in a southerly direction along Dundalk Street. The line of the wall is difficult to trace at this point, but it probably turned eastwards and followed the route of the graveyard wall which surrounds the Holy Trinity church, leaving the Dominican friary outside the precinct of the town. Turn left up the little path that follows the mill race to the mill, a nineteenth-century ruined building. In 1211 the pipe roll of King John records payments for a mill and mill-pond at Carlingford and the present mill probably occupies the site of the older structure. The mill became the property of the friars and must have been a valuable source of income for them. The remains of the friary lie to the north-west in an adjacent field. It was founded in 1305 by Richard de Burgh, earl of Ulster, and consists of a church building with a nave and chancel and a later bell tower. The domestic buildings extended southwards from the chancel and there is slight evidence for a cloistered walkway. The south and north walls of the church have parapets and a machicolation protects the west doorway, evidence of the independent nature of this pious community in an era of political turmoil. It was dissolved by Henry VIII in the 1530s and by 1543 it was being used as accommodation for 'those who resort to the place in large numbers with the fleet of ships every year to catch herrings and other fish'. In 1671 the site became the subject of a struggle for repossession between the Dominicans and the Franciscans, a dispute which was settled by Oliver Plunkett in favour of the Dominicans. The friary was finally abandoned by the order in the eighteenth century.

In 1237 Hugh de Lacy granted the profits of the churches of Carlingford and Rooskey to St Andrew's church in Scotland. The remains of the church at Rooskey are still visible to the south-west of the town, and it is very likely that the church at Carlingford occupied the site of the present day Holy Trinity Heritage Centre, formerly a Church of Ireland church. Fifteenth-century documentary sources refer to four churches within the liberties of the town, 'the church of the Holy Trinity, the parish church of St Mary, the church at Rooskey and the chapel at St Michael'. Evidence from a map dated 1624 indicates that the last of these may have occupied a site south of the town which is still referred to as Chapel Field or Hospital Field. Perhaps it functioned in association with a hospital in the medieval period. However, it is the church of the Holy Trinity that survives today, greatly altered and modified through the ages. As we walk back towards the town from the friary we are afforded an excellent view of it on its lofty position, on a ridge which overlooks the harbour and the town. It is surrounded by a graveyard which is inter-denominational and contains a number of interesting grave-stones. Two markers may date to the fifteenth century but the earliest inscribed stone dates to 1703.

We leave the graveyard through its east gate and turn left towards the Tholsel. 'Tholsel' is an old English word which roughly translates as a meeting hall or place where tolls were collected. Tholsels were usually located in the market square of medieval towns, but in Carlingford it is the name associated with the last surviving town gate. This particular building has had a number of functions, such as a toll gate, the sessions house of the corporation in the seventeenth century and the town jail in the eighteenth century. In fact, it is reputed to have once accommodated a parliament which made laws for the whole of the Pale.

Carlingford had developed an administrative framework in the form of a corporation and we are particularly fortunate to have a roll of its sovereigns and burgesses from 1706 to 1828 and minutes of the corporation for the same period. However the corporation of Carlingford is much older than these records indicate. It dates back to at least 1326 and to the first recorded charter granted to the bailiffs of the town. A number of other charters were granted over the years providing permission for customs and by-laws, a weekly market, the creation of a free borough, the organisation and appointment of the officers of the corporation, and the allocation of rights, privileges and duties. The corporation had its own seal; its motif has been resurrected and is a popular symbol for many groups in the town today.

The narrow slightly curving street that leads us back towards the square is called Tholsel Street and it requires very little imagination to picture what it would have looked like on a typical market day in the fifteenth or sixteenth century. The imagination is aided by the presence of the Mint, a fifteenth-century fortified town house, a fine example of a well-to-do merchant's residence, home and business premises to one of the families that controlled the town's medieval trade. Its most interesting features are its five highly decorated limestone windows which are a sixteenth-century insertion and are an example of the influence of the Celtic renaissance on art in this period. In 1467 the town was granted the right to mint coinage, but coins were never minted in this building as it does not contain the architectural features required for such an industry. The name was probably placed on the building by some romantic antiquarian who sought to create a tangible link with the 1467 licence. Coins from Carlingford have never come to light but an act of parliament granting this privilege indicates the town's importance as a regional trading and administrative centre at the time.

Carlingford is fortunate to have yet another example of a wealthy merchant's residence in Taaffe's Castle, one of the finest medieval fortified town houses in Ireland. It is located to the north-east of the square and once stood on the old harbour front. The lane which extends southwards from Taaffe's and parallel to Tholsel Street is called Old Quay Lane and has a number of warehouses dating from the eighteenth century fronting onto it. But let us return our attention to Taaffe's. This sixteenth-century construction had quite a sophisticated plan; the ground floor consisted of a large vaulted storage chamber which opened directly on to the shoreline and the upper floors contained the living quarters with en suite toilets, glazed windows, window seats, stone fireplaces and separate kitchens. The Mint and Taaffe's Castle are reminders of Carlingford's position as an important trading port on the east coast of Ireland, utilising the busy Irish Sea trade routes.

By the middle of the thirteenth century, Carlingford's sea trade had developed sufficiently for it to be numbered amongst the ports of Ulster along with Dundalk, Strangford, Carrickfergus and Coleraine. The sheltered, well-protected harbour and the wealth of herrings and oysters in the lough formed the economic basis of the town's continued existence throughout the medieval period.

The medieval town possessed at least two more town houses located at the upper end of Newry Street, towards King John's castle. Evidence for these sites are in the remains of a gable end on the left and the vaulted basement of another directly across the street. As we walk towards these sites we are reminded of nineteenth-century development by the presence of the town hall, courthouse, old coastguard station, and Presbyterian church which form a continual line on the left. Our tour finishes back at King John's castle which, to this day, dominates the town and the harbour. Land reclamation and a new road have interfered with the intimate relationship between the town and the harbour but otherwise, as we look back over the settlement, we can see how the town, in essence, is still confined within the old medieval limits. Development outside the town walls dates from the early eighteenth century, such as Ghan House, 'ghan' meaning 'poor land by the sea', which is situated to the south-east of the Tholsel. It is a fine example of a rural mansion of the middle gentry. Other buildings include the manse to the west, the rectory, Catholic church, national school and two small 1950s housing estates to the south, and, of course, the ubiquitous bungalows dotted along the Greenore road and on the gentler slopes of the mountain.

Having flourished in the medieval period the town went into decline after 1600. A more direct inland route from Leinster to Ulster via the Moyry pass was used after the suppression of the northern Gaelic lords and the old coastal route via Carlingford was increasingly by-passed. The town was directly affected by the political turmoil of the seventeenth century. Many of the old families were dispossessed after the rebellion of 1641. Phelim O'Neill ordered the place to be burned in 1642 and William of Orange used the harbour for his supply ships in 1689 and 1690. The Williamite general, the duke of Schomberg, sent his fever-stricken soldiers to Carlingford to wait on hospital ships from Carrickfergus. Its political importance did not automatically bring prosperity and the 1677 'Roden Title', a description of property owned by the earl of Roden, records many vacant plots in the town. Carlingford's economy was further undermined when Dundalk was developed by the Hamilton family. The construction of a canal into the new town of Newry to the north brought trade which was traditionally Carlingford's further into the northern heartland. The shoals of herring which came every year to the lough shifted to the open seas, bringing the fishing fleets with them. But the town still continued to function as a port. A short pier was built in the late eighteenth century and by the mid-nineteenth century exports to England and Wales included quarried limestone from Slieve Foy, potatoes from Cooley and fish from the lough; in fact, the Carlingford oyster was considered quite a delicacy in Europe at the time. The quarries also supplied stone for the construction of the Dundalk, Greenore and Newry railway line which opened in 1876. The line followed a route along the town's seafront and necessitated the in-filling of the old quay and the construction of the two piers which now enclose the harbour.

Yet despite these advances Carlingford never developed an industry. The sea trade business moved to Greenore where the deep-water facilities were more suitable for the requirements of a modern port. There was a short-lived postwar economic boom, but the fortunes of the town went into rapid decline with the advent of the political problems in the north. When many towns underwent radical changes in the prosperous 1960s and 1970s Carlingford remained a little place that functioned mainly as a dormitory town to Dundalk and Newry. This lack of development in an era which is unfortunately synonymous with bad taste and bad planning by chance preserved the very features which give Carlingford its special atmosphere and character.

From the late 1970s the community was revitalised through the activities of various organisations such as the community council, the Oyster Co-op, the tourism and festivals committee, the pipe band, the Red Cross, the Credit Union and the Heritage Trust. The Tidy Towns committee succeeded in winning the national Tidy Towns award in 1988 and has won the county award for twelve years in succession. The Heritage Trust was formed in 1990 and has been successful in sourcing grant aid for a number of restoration and redevelopment projects. The town is included in Bord Failte's heritage towns programme and the trust received a substantial grant from them for the development of a heritage centre in the Holy Trinity church, the floodlighting of King John's castle, the repair of the Tholsel, and a number of publications on the history of the town. With grant aid from the International Fund for Ireland the trust purchased, and is in the process of developing, a derelict site on Tholsel Street. FÁS have been used on a number of schemes such as repairs to the Holy Trinity graveyard, the mill and mill pond and the fragment of the medieval town wall, and the construction of a dry stone wall on the Greenore road. The office of public works began the restoration of the Dominican friary in 1990.

The success of the various community groups has encouraged the private sector to invest in the improvement of the fabric of the town. Ghan House is being restored and the out-buildings have been converted into an equestrian centre. An old grain store on Dundalk Street has also been restored by its owner and presently houses a language school, coffee shop and two shop units. Craft shops are opening, guesthouses are adding rooms to their premises, and numerous old houses have been repaired.

But not all of the properties have been treated with the sensitivity they deserve. The vernacular Georgian facade of Carlingford is rapidly disappearing as not enough attention is given to detail. The planning authorities have no development plan for Carlingford, and there is an urgent need for one. In the meantime it is to be hoped that people will become more enlightened through the attention given to this subject and by the example of a number of carefully restored properties in the town itself.

Frontier towns have never had an easy existence. Economic vulnerability is, at present, the major obstacle for small border communities in the south to overcome. Carlingford has awoken from its long slumber. It is a vital place with a community which has the nerve to take on the challenge of developing its economic and cultural life without detracting from its intimate character. The Irish scholar, Fr Laurence Murray, a son of Carlingford, wrote: 'there is a medieval suggestiveness about it that carries one back many centuries and fills the mind with vague dreamings.' It is as apt a description today as when it was written in 1914.

Select bibliography
H. G. Tempest: 'The roll of the sovereigns and burgesses of Carlingford, 1706-1828', *County Louth Archaeological and Historical Journal*, iii (3) (1914), pp. 273-87
T. J. Hughes: 'Landholding and settlement in the Cooley peninsula of Louth', *Irish Geography*, iv (1961), pp. 149-74
A. Curran: 'The Dominican order in Carlingford and Dundalk', *County Louth Archaeological and Historical Journal*, xvi (3) (1967), pp. 143-60
H. Tempest: *Guide to County Louth*, Dundalk, 1983
Office of Public Works: *Archaeological Survey of County Louth*, Dublin, 1991
P. Gosling: *Carlingford Town: an Antiquarian's Guide*, Carlingford, 1992

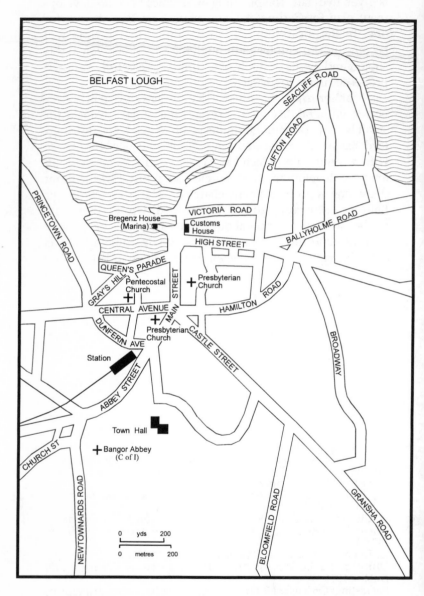

Bangor, based on Ordnance Survey Road Atlas of Ireland, 1985

BANGOR

Philip Robinson

BANGOR, in North Down, occupies one of the oldest town sites in Ireland. It can trace its origin to the founding of Bangor abbey by St Comgall about A.D. 555. Indeed early missionaries from Bangor played such a prominent role in the Christianisation of Europe, that by the middle ages it was one of only four Irish sites named in the famous *mappa mundi* or map of the world completed about 1314. This map is now to be found in Hereford cathedral, and the other three sites marked were Armagh, Dublin and Kildare.

Today, Bangor is the fourth largest town in Northern Ireland, and is only 12 miles from Belfast, the largest. It has a population of about 46,000, many of whom have only recently come to live in the greatly expanded suburbs. It has long been a favoured dormitory town for the Belfast business and professional classes but, in recent years, large developments of public and private sector housing have provided re-location possibilities for a large number of Belfast people of all classes.

The seafront of Bangor extends four miles along the southern shore of Belfast Lough, and is broken into two distinct bays by a promontory. The sandy bay to the east is known as Ballyholme Bay, while the main focus of the town is on the natural harbour in Bangor Bay itself. Since the last century, Bangor has been a popular holiday centre so that it now has many of the characteristics of a Victorian 'day-trip' resort.

Sandwiched between the emergence of Bangor as an important Early Christian settlement, and its nineteenth-century personality as a holiday and retirement resort is another important epoch of the town's history. During the Ulster plantation of the early seventeenth century, Bangor was transformed by Sir James Hamilton from a much-declined late medieval village into one of the most thriving

Bangor, harbour and waterfront in 1854, from J. B. Doyle, Towns in Ulster

plantation centres in Ulster.

As might be expected with any settlement site on the north-east coast of Ireland, its most important periods of expansion were coincidental with increased international contact and increased maritime trade and activity in and across the North Channel. The arrival and spread of Christianity in the fifth and sixth centuries marked one such period of sea-based contact for north-east Ireland. St Patrick's arrival, and his earliest mission in south-east Down, was clearly part of such a process, and the popular perception of his association with the Ulaid in east Ulster is reinforced by his reputed burial at Downpatrick rather than at Armagh.

Controversy has been evoked in recent years over the ethnicity of the Ulaid at that time, some even asserting that they were essentially a Cruithin or Pictish people rather than Gaels. While this may be an over-statement, the area of north Down where Bangor is located was then the territory of the Dál Riada, a sept of the Ulaid who were undisputedly

Cruithin.

The founder of Bangor as a monastic site was St Comgall, the son of Setna – a supposed Pictish warrior living in east Antrim. He was born at Magheramourne in 517, only a generation after St Patrick's mission. Comgall founded an abbey of regular canons at Bangor about the year 555 and his monastery soon expanded to include hundreds – some say thousands – of monks. They established a school that quickly became one of the most celebrated seminaries in Europe. The three great lights of Christianity in the British Isles in the sixth century are often cited as Iona, Bangor in County Down, and Bangor in Wales. In fact there were two Bangor foundations in Wales – the Caernarvonshire Bangor which was founded about 520 and the more famous Flintshire Bangor in 547. There was no direct relationship between the Flintshire Bangor and the Irish abbey of the same name, but all these great religious houses were interconnected. Our Bangor became known as 'Bangor Mor' or Great Bangor, to distinguish it from the Welsh monastic sites.

In the Welsh language, the word 'Bangor' is thought to have had a meaning associated with the construction of circular wattle fences or huts, while Irish Gaelic scholars have long debated different possible derivations. Many legends have also been collected which purport to explain the origin of the name. Some nineteenth-century antiquarians took Bangor to mean 'white choir', while more recent scholars have preferred derivations involving *beann*, a prefix understood to mean 'peak' or a 'horn'. In the recently published volume of *Place Names of Northern Ireland* relating to the Ards, the authors suggest reconciling the later interpretation of *beann*, meaning a horn, to the Welsh *ban*, meaning a band used to strengthen something such as in wattling. Thus *beannchor* could refer to the type of fence constructed with prongs surrounding the monastic site, and subsequently may have come to mean the site itself within any such enclosure.

The County Down monastery was indeed within a large circular enclosure which included the present site of the abbey church and probably extended behind it to cover a portion of Cross Hill. Cross Hill was part of a larger rise between Ballyholme Bay to the east and the natural harbour at Bangor Bay to the west, and is dominated today by Bangor castle. A small stream known as Beg or Bec flowed around the lower edge of the early monastic site and then along the line of the present main street, falling steeply over about a quarter of a mile to the sea-front at Bangor Bay. The early name of Bangor was Inver Bec or 'the mouth of the Bec'. It was in this stream that St Comgall was believed to immerse himself each night to recite psalms. About 565 St Comgall accompanied St Columba of Iona and St Canice of Kilkenny on their mission to the Pictish king of east Scotland at Inverness. Comgall was a close friend of Columba and their role on this mission was to act as interpreters. St Comgall died in 602 and was buried at Bangor.

For several centuries, until the early 800s, the monastery at Bangor retained its status as one of the most important Early Christian schools and missionary centres in northern Europe. This period, however, was followed by one of rapid decline early in the ninth century, with the onset of Viking raids. About A.D. 800 the first attack by the Danes occurred and ten years later, in another raid, the tomb of Comgall was broken open and his relics scattered. In some of these raids, hundreds of monks were reported to have been slain, a fact which in itself testifies to the size and importance of the settlement. Unlike the Early Christian settlement sites around Strangford Lough in County Down, the decline in the importance of Bangor continued throughout the late ninth, tenth and eleventh centuries.

There is some evidence that the Danes had begun to settle and become christianised at places like Nendrum and Downpatrick. Paradoxically, following their initial raids during the ninth century, the only Viking burial in Ulster to have yielded material evidence, was discovered at Ballyholme Bay beside Bangor. Indeed the 'holme' element in Ballyholme is considered to be a Viking place-name element. The Irish annals of the eleventh century confirm that most of the recorded activity in east Down was focused on the 'foreigners of Lough Cuan' – a euphemism for the Vikings of

Strangford Lough. The Ulaid, including the men of Dál Riada, fought against Brian Boru, on the side of the Vikings, at the battle of Clontarf in 1016. In 1065, Donnchadh, king of Ulaid, was slain by the Ulaid themselves in the stone church of Bangor. Before this date, there is no suggestion of any stone buildings at the famous monastery settlement, and this reference is often taken to be an error, given that a century later St Malachy was credited with building the first stone church here.

In 1124 St Malachy was appointed as the abbot of Bangor. He had been born in Armagh in 1095 and had developed a considerable reputation as a church leader. St Malachy was simultaneously appointed bishop of Connor, a diocese that comprised the territories of Dál Riada and Ulaid, so that Bangor became his episcopal seat. Malachy first of all built a wooden oratory of 'smooth planks closely fastened together'. What appeared to have been the possibility of a revival in the fortunes of Bangor was interrupted in 1127, when the monastery was attacked by Connor O'Loughlin, king of the northern O'Neills, during which the so-called city of Bangor was destroyed. Following this, Malachy, with 130 monks, left Bangor and by 1134 had become archbishop at Armagh. However, by 1137, Malachy resigned at Armagh to return to Bangor, where he re-established the monastery and began preparing for a major missionary journey to the continent. On his return from Europe, he caused a stone church to be built at Bangor, supposedly in imitation of the churches he had seen on the continent. Because of this St Malachy has been described as a pioneer of Hiberno-Romanesque architecture in Ireland. Unfortunately no evidence survives at Bangor today for any structures built before or during this period.

The arrival of the Anglo-Normans at the end of the twelfth century was to herald four centuries of monastic building and urban settlement development in east Ulster. However, again the eclipse of Bangor continued in terms of its relative importance, compared to other east Ulster centres. Various monastic orders were introduced into Ireland at this time and the Augustinians became responsible for Bangor. The oldest remains within the present abbey church date from the fourteenth century. The tower, now at the entrance, was originally the central tower of a magnificent Augustinian church. The only other material evidence from the fourteenth century is the beautifully decorated Bangor bell, which survives in pristine condition in a local museum collection. The 1367 statute of Kilkenny, which refused permission to any mere Irishman to make his profession in a religious house situated among the English, was applied to Bangor.

During the medieval period, other monastic orders associated with the Anglo-Normans had simultaneously developed larger and more enduring abbeys, such as the Cistercians at Greyabbey and Inch abbey. In terms of secular building, the potential Bangor had to develop as a medieval town attached to the abbey site, was completely overshadowed by the decision of John de Courcy to develop Carrickfergus, on the opposite shore of Belfast Lough in County Antrim, as the principal strategic centre for the Anglo-Normans in Ulster. By 1469 the church buildings had fallen into disuse and responsibility for the site was transferred to the Franciscans.

So it was that when the reformation came to Ireland in the sixteenth century, its limited effect was more immediately apparent in places like Carrickfergus, where economic and church activity was centred. The dissolution of the monasteries took effect in Bangor in 1542, when the last abbot, William O'Dornan, surrendered the abbey along with over 30 townlands then in its possession throughout north Down. The reign of Queen Elizabeth witnessed the beginning of a new era in Ireland, the age of plantation, and this was to prove the beginning of a major new epoch in the development of Bangor as an urban settlement.

Towards the end of the medieval period, the area of Anglo-Norman control had contracted drastically. In the 1380s a series of incursions by the Tyrone O'Neills into south Antrim and north Down effectively split the earldom of Ulster in two. These 'Clandeboye' O'Neills, so called after Clan Hugh Boy O'Neill, were perceived by the last of the

Tudors, Elizabeth I, to have usurped crown lands. In the early 1570s, Sir Thomas Smith, the queen's secretary of state, along with his illegitimate son Thomas, devised a scheme for the plantation of the Ards. Originally this Smith plantation was to be of the entire Clandeboye territories held by Sir Brian MacPhelim O'Neill in south Antrim and north Down. It was soon realised however that the Smith venture could only in practice deal with north Down and the Ards peninsula, while the earl of Essex was to further his own plantation scheme in County Antrim.

The earl of Essex's Antrim plantation was launched from the secure base of the English-controlled town of Carrickfergus. The Smith colonists were to land at Strangford village in south-east Down – an area densely populated still with 'Old English' or descendants of the Anglo-Normans. Sir Brian MacPhelim O'Neill burned the abbeys at Bangor, Newtownards, Comber and Greyabbey so that none of these could afford shelter for Smith's plantation venture. The limited success of this scheme had virtually no impact on Bangor itself, for the Smith colonists only established themselves in the Ards peninsula and the Comber-Newtownards area.

In 1589 the land still under the effective control of the Clandeboye O'Neills passed to Con McBrien Fertagh O'Neill, the last of the chiefs of Clandeboye. Almost at the same time as the death of Elizabeth in 1603 and the crowning of James VI of Scotland as James I of England and Scotland, Con O'Neill was arrested on a spurious charge, following a brawl between some of his followers and English soldiers at Castlereagh. Sir James Hamilton and Sir Hugh Montgomery were at this time two Scots in very good standing at the court of James I. They conspired with a somewhat gullible Con O'Neill to effect his release and pardon through the re-granting of all the County Down Clandeboye lands between all three of them. Although the estates involved were enormous and fragmented, Con O'Neill's land was centred around Castlereagh to the west, Montgomery's around Newtownards and Sir James Hamilton's at Bangor. So this Ayrshire laird then became the founder of the modern town of Bangor, that is if a plantation town commenced in 1605 can indeed be described as a modern town. Hamilton made Bangor his family seat and built a large stone house on the site of the present Victorian building still known as Bangor castle. In 1612, James I granted borough status to Bangor, giving the corporation the right to return two members of parliament. By this date the town contained 80 new houses built for the Scottish and English settlers. The only surviving plantation building from this period in Bangor is the customs house, built by Sir James Hamilton beside the harbour. The customs house is a dominant landmark on the seafront. It has tower-house proportions, with crow-step gabling on a corner turret.

The old abbey site effectively became the parish church at this period and in 1617 the ruined church was rebuilt to include the fifteenth-century tower. The majority of the settlers in Bangor were Scots rather than English, and in 1609 Hamilton had brought over from Scotland a curate for the church called John Gibson. Following Gibson's death, another Scot, Robert Blair, was appointed in 1623. He was not only a Presbyterian but strongly opposed to the episcopacy. Blair's exploits as a Presbyterian advocate within the established church became legendary in Ulster until 1636, when he attempted to sail for America in the *Eagle's Wing*. This ship, like Columbanus' vessel a millennium before, foundered in a storm and Blair went back to Scotland. As he was not only a Presbyterian, but also a covenanter, we should remember that he had in fact been minister of the abbey church itself in Bangor.

The early plantation town of Bangor itself was described in the report of the plantation commissioners in 1611 as follows:

Sir James Hamilton, Knight, hath builded a fair stone house at the town of Bangor, in the Upper Clandeboye, within the county aforesaid, about 60 foot long and 22 foot broad; the town consists of 80 new houses, all inhabited with Scotsmen and Englishmen. And hath brought out of England 20 artificers, who are making materials of timber, brick, and stone, for another house there.

The 80 or so houses mentioned in this report appear in a map of the town and its neighbourhood prepared in 1625. This shows almost all the development at the seafront in Bangor Bay and along two major streets running inland from the seafront. At the west end of the bay, the largest street clearly links the abbey site to the harbour. In effect it is the earliest representation of the present Main Street. Slightly to the east another street is shown along the line of what is now High Street. Hamilton's own castle, or 'fair stone house', is marked at the top of Main Street but is set back within its own parks and sandwiched between this new town on one side and the abbey church and site to the other.

This map was prepared by Thomas Raven, the city of London's surveyor, who was commissioned to complete a survey of the entire Hamilton estates in north Down while he was in Ulster to prepare similar surveys for the London companies in County Londonderry. It seems evident from the map of Bangor, prepared by Raven, that the morphology of the new town of Bangor was already established many centuries before. A water-mill is shown in the town at the mouth of a small river, beside the harbour, and just outside the 1625 town limits are shown a rabbit warren and a bowling green.

The charter of incorporation for Bangor provided for a weekly market, and stated that there was to be a provost, twelve free burgesses and an unlimited number of freemen for the town. Within a few years of the start of the plantation, Bangor town and the surrounding countryside had become densely settled by great numbers of Scots. In 1630, all major landowners in Ulster were required to return a muster roll of their British tenants capable of bearing arms. Lord Clandeboye, as Sir James Hamilton had become, returned over 500 names of adult males in the parish of Bangor. This was by far the largest single return in Ulster, and the overwhelming majority of these names were lowland Scots rather than English. Clearly however these tenants were not all townsmen, for the 80 houses recorded in Bangor town in 1611 probably were much the same as the 97 households recorded for the 'corporation of Bangor' in a

1659 poll tax list.

In 1637, the surveyor general, Charles Moncke, reported on customs in the northern ports of Ireland. Writing from Bangor on 16 September, he recorded:

> I have now passed the Clandeboyes, which is a large country altogether inhabited by Scots, the customs there in Donaghadee and Bangor being raised for the most part by cattle... The lord of Clandeboye is building of another goodly house at Bangor which will be one of the first in the kingdom ... There is a fair custom house built but not finished by the lord of Clandeboye who hath received between two and three hundred pounds of the king towards it. It is a large pile of stone made with flankers and might serve as well for the defence of the harbour. If it were finished it were the best customs house in Ireland.

The plantation town remained about the same size throughout the seventeenth century. Indeed a detailed map of Bangor for 1757 shows little growth and almost no change in the layout by the middle of the eighteenth century. The seafront development is called Sandy Row or Raa and a corn-mill is still shown on this map beside the harbour. Between this and the customs house a meeting house is marked, revealing that the Presbyterians had become a separate denomination in Bangor after the mid-seventeenth century. The first of the two principal streets marked in 1625 is shown in 1757 as Ballymagee Street, a name retained until the late nineteenth century, since when it has been known as High Street. The most important street is marked as Market Street and this coincides with today's Main Street. Further inland along Main Street some houses had been developed around the abbey, particularly along Church Street. This area is now called Abbey Street and is almost half a mile from the seafront. In 1757 Hamilton's castle still occupied the higher ground between the abbey and the plantation town. This map shows about 130 tenement plots associated with individual buildings in the town. Allowing for the fact that some 30 of these are shown in a new nucleus around the old abbey site, the plantation town could have changed very little since 1611.

Another century on, in the 1830s, Bangor was again

surveyed in detail. A valuation map of 1834 begins to show some growth of the town. At the seafront Sandy Row had been extended west into the new housing at Grey's Hill, and seafront terraces had been built on the site of the 1625 rabbit warren. At the east end of Bangor Bay the town had begun to extend along a street called Fisher's Hill over the promontory separating the harbour from Ballyholme Bay. A considerable number of houses had also been built by 1834 around the abbey site, almost as a separate development. This area, now known as Abbey Street, was then called Church Quarter, and included other new terraced houses built off this road along Church Street and Croft Street. The development in this area had still not coalesced with that of the rest of the town at the head of Main Street by the middle of the nineteenth century, and so it was on this last remaining green area that the railway station was built in 1865.

Bangor town in 1837 consisted of about 550 houses, and Main Street was described as being the chief seat of local trade, containing the principal shops, a couple of schools, market-house, corn mill and the so-called 'First' Presbyterian church. This Presbyterian church was in fact built in 1831 in Main Street at the same time as another meeting house close to Church Quarter and the abbey. The first meeting house building actually constructed in Bangor was marked on the 1757 map beside the customs house and harbour, and was still used as a Presbyterian meeting house in the 1830s.

The population of Bangor fell from just over 3,000 in 1841 to 2,850 in 1851. This decline continued well after the famine years until 1871 when the population had dropped to 2,560. However following the introduction of the railway, the development of Bangor as a late Victorian seaside resort and residential town was reflected in its population growth between 1881 (when it was again only about 3,000) until 1901, when the population had virtually doubled to almost 6,000. In the middle of the nineteenth century, the population of Bangor parish as a whole numbered 9,365, of which 8,230 were Presbyterians, 761 belonged to the established church and Roman Catholics numbered 251. By the end of the century, with the influx of great numbers of business and professional people from Belfast, the overwhelming dominance of Presbyterians in the town was somewhat modified by an increase in the proportion of other denominations, particularly Church of Ireland, and this trend has continued down to the present.

In recent years the entire southern or landward side of Bangor has been encircled by a dual carriageway known locally as the Bangor 'ring road'. Modern housing developments flank both sides of this road, and it is punctuated by a series of roundabouts marking the intersection of older roads leading into the town. The appearance of the town as a modern dormitory settlement for Belfast is the first impression any visitor will receive on approaching the town. These developments however surround a commercial core which mostly retains the basic morphology of the historic town.

Within the past few years a major and somewhat controversial transformation of the seafront has taken place. The construction of an enormous marina complex for yachts, along with a substantial new building to house marina offices and coastguard facilities, has had an enormous impact on the appearance of the sea frontage. The building has been named Bregenz House in honour of one of the abbey's early European missions, and indeed it is possible to view these recreational developments at the harbour as a natural continuation of the town's more recent heritage as a popular holiday and leisure venue. However, the material evidence of Bangor's past, in terms of surviving buildings, provides only a poor shadow of the town's lengthy and important history.

Select bibliography
A. Knox: *A History of the County Down*, Dublin, 1875
J. Stevenson: *Two Centuries of Life in Down 1600-1800*, Belfast, 1920
I. Adamson: *Bangor Light of the World*, Belfast, 1979
J. Hamilton: *Bangor Abbey through Fourteen Centuries*, Belfast, 1980
Journal of the Bangor Historical Society, 1981 –
M. Patton: *Historic Buildings: Bangor and Groomsport*, Belfast, 1984

COLERAINE

Raymond Gillespie

FOR the traveller from Belfast bound for the seaside resort of Portrush on the north Antrim coast the town of Coleraine, formerly an important landmark on his journey, is now all too easy to ignore. The 1740 turnpike road which used to pass through the town has been improved by a by-pass which confines the view of Coleraine to the steel chimneys of the University of Ulster, built just outside the town in the 1970s. Approaching from the Derry side of the town through the plantation settlement of Macosquin the visitor gets a rather different impression. The road from the west passes through the straggling nineteenth-century suburb of Killowen before crossing the bridge over the River Bann and after a short journey up Bridge Street the traveller arrives in the town square, the Diamond. In the centre of the Diamond, and dominating it, is Thomas Turner's town hall built in 1859 at a cost of £4,146. Here is evidence of a solidly prosperous Victorian town and indeed that is what modern-day Coleraine is. The buildings erected around the Diamond in the nineteenth century by banks provide further evidence of modest Victorian prosperity. The values of the age are proclaimed on the facade of a Victorian shop at 23 Waterford Place with the words: 'the hand of the diligent worketh right'.

In 1841, four years after Queen Victoria came to the throne, Coleraine was the sixth largest town in Ulster with 6,255 souls. In the year she died, 1901, Coleraine had a population of 7,785 although it had slipped in the ranking of Ulster towns to ninth, pushed down by the growth of surrounding towns such as Ballymena and Larne. Yet the townscape indicates that it maintained its prosperity and it still reveals many of the preoccupations of Victorian society in Coleraine. Most of the churches in the town date from the reign of Queen Victoria. Some, such as the Methodist church,

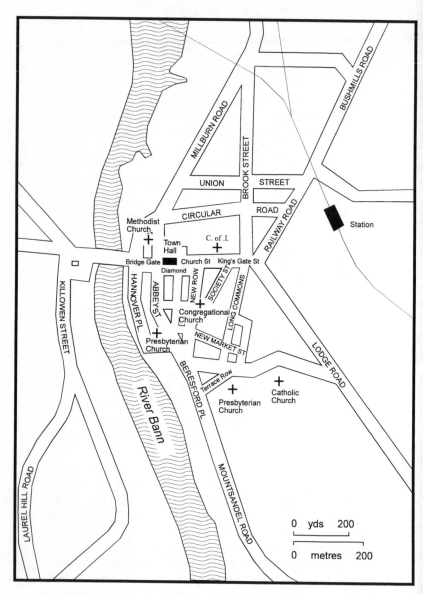

Coleraine, based on Ordnance Survey Road Atlas of Ireland, 1985

built in 1853, were rebuilt as a result of greater prosperity. The first Methodist church, built in 1801 at a cost of £500, was replaced with a grander structure costing £2,540. The Church of Ireland also took advantage of prosperity to demolish the old church, which had been patched and enlarged several times since 1611. It was replaced by the present structure in 1884. Coleraine was, however, decidedly a Presbyterian town with almost two-thirds of its population adhering to that church in 1831. The Presbyterians, too, rose to the challenge of modernisation. In 1833 the First Presbyterian church in Abbey Street added its Doric portico, New Row refronted its structure with an Italianate stucco front in 1891 and the Terrace Row congregation added a flamboyant classical front in the following year. This was not the first alteration to Terrace Row Presbyterian church. It had been enlarged in 1860 to accommodate new members following the evangelical revival of 1859. Coleraine adopted the call to evangelical respectability and sales of improving literature such as the *Presbyterian Penny Magazine*, the *Orthodox Presbyterian* and the *Sabbath School Magazine* boomed in the town during the 1830s.

Roman Catholics were a much smaller proportion of the population in Victorian Coleraine, less than 15 per cent in 1831, but they too made their impact on the townscape. Relaxation of the penal code and the passing of Catholic emancipation saw Catholic clergy, absent from the town since the seventeenth century, return and begin construction of churches. First on the Killowen side of the river, St John's church went up in 1834 and in 1836 one was built in the town itself.

The Victorians' cult of respectability and improvement did not stop with churches. Their preoccupation with poor relief and education both made an impact on the townscape. The Irish poor law made provision for workhouses and one was built at Coleraine in 1841 on the site of the present Coleraine hospital. It is now demolished except for the five-bay, two-storeyed governor's house. Such state involvement replaced a series of private local philanthropic schemes. In 1834 the Coleraine Poor House and Mendicity Association,

St Patrick's parish church, Coleraine, 1816

established in 1825, supported 161 poor in their own homes. A workhouse, established in 1830, cared for 33 persons who were employed in breaking stones and spinning. The story of education in the town is similar. There were private and public schools as well as Sunday schools in the town before the commissioners of national education built their school in 1847. This older tradition of voluntary education did not die easily. In 1860 Coleraine Academical Institute was established with an impressive building, happily still there but much enlarged.

Above all, Victorian Coleraine's prosperity was based on trade and on services to meet the needs of the surrounding countryside. As the Ordnance Survey memoir of the early 1830s noted, all the depositors in Coleraine's Savings Bank were farmers. The town provided an unusually wide range of services for its hinterland. If the occupations recorded in the parish register are a guide, farmers could come to Coleraine for a haircut, to make a will, to have a clock made or repaired, to buy new shoes, to have a new suit cut, to visit the apothecary or to buy some of the latest luxuries from Dublin. They could also have their corn ground in the new mill, built in 1831, which used the latest milling technology imported from Scotland. The town also had a farming society, set up in 1821, which encouraged farmers to improve the standard of agriculture by competing in annual ploughing matches or cattle shows.

However, it was as a place for buying and selling agricultural produce that Coleraine was most important. The New Market, built in 1830 in New Market Street and still surviving, provided a Saturday market for grain, potatoes, butter and flax. This surviving market is only a reminder of the many markets scattered through the Victorian town. The Shambles, off Bridge Street, was a meat and fish market and every Saturday an open-air linen market was held in the Diamond with a yarn market in Church Street. A weekly cattle market was held in a field near the town. These markets provided farmers with access to a wider world for their produce. It is easy to forget that the Victorian trading town of Coleraine was also a port, albeit not a very good one. A shifting sand bar across the mouth of the River Bann made access to the town from the coast difficult but the building of a harbour at Portrush, about five miles from Coleraine, between 1827 and 1836 created an outport for the town. By the 1830s 160 ships were trading from the port taking out grain (mainly oats), bacon, pork and butter and bringing in coal, tea, iron and sugar. One local speciality was seasonally important in this trade, the Bann salmon which were sent to Liverpool in large quantities. Further links with the outside world were established in 1855 with the coming of the railway and by 1860 the town was linked to the rapidly growing industrial town of Belfast. Coleraine may have been a provincial town but it expected to be in touch with the outside world through the railway, the port, or the London, Liverpool, Glasgow and Belfast newspapers which could be found in the news room in the town hall. For the more affluent there were the periodicals sold in the town which in the 1830s included the *Magazine of Fashion,*

Blackwood's Magazine, the *Encyclopaedia Britannica* and the *London Gardens Magazine.*

On the face of it therefore Coleraine is the exemplar of a modestly prosperous Ulster town of the nineteenth century. The pride of the inhabitants is revealed in the comment of the 1830s that 'the general style of the streets is broad and they are well laid out. The town has a neat and clean appearance'. Yet this comment creates unease in the inquisitive observer and this would be magnified by even a cursory walk around the town. The streets are just too broad and too well laid out to be the result of organic growth in the nineteenth century. They radiate from the Diamond in a planned grid-iron way reminiscent of Derry. The town has all the appearance of a planned town with a central guiding hand in its creation. In fact it is a planned town and its Victorian appearance says little about its origins. As the archetypal schoolboy knows Coleraine is a textbook example of one of those planned towns, such as Bandon, set up in the early seventeenth century by landlords on estates newly acquired as part of the plantations and colonisation of that era. In contrast to Bandon, however, the landlord in the case of Coleraine was not an individual but a new-fangled invention of the seventeenth century, a joint stock company. As part of the scheme for the plantation of Ulster, County Londonderry was to be settled by a group of twelve London livery companies who established a holding company, the Irish Society, to provide the basic infrastructure for the settlement, including the two port towns of Derry and Coleraine. The surviving evidence of the Irish Society's involvement with the town is meagre but its influence was real. Society Street, for instance, takes its name from it and the names of its agents are preserved in Beresford Place and Waterford Place. The society also endowed a school in the town.

In the original scheme the society was to build the town and lease it to settlers and they are responsible for the planned appearance of the townscape. Originally they were to build 100 houses and leave space for 200 more within an area which they were to enclose with a rampart. This wall, six feet high and made of turf and earth with a timber palisade fence on top, enclosed five sides with the river being the sixth side of the town. From the river it extended briefly south before turning to follow the line of Society Street, formerly known as the Rampart, whose erratic course is out of keeping with the rest of the town because it follows the original line of the wall. It turned north-east by St Patrick's church, where a portion of the original rampart survives, and passed by the end of Rosemary Lane and Bell House Lane before reaching the river on the northern side of the town. There were three gates, now remembered only in the street names Kingsgate and Bridgegate, and outside the walls lay the common land on which the townsmen could graze their cattle, now recalled in the street known as Long Commons.

By 1611 work was under way and most of the town resembled a building site when Sir George Carew visited it in that year. 379 workmen were employed, carpenters, brick-layers, slaters, brickmakers, carters and labourers being the most common. 600,000 bricks had already been fired as had 56,000 tiles and timber was being brought from the sur-rounding woods to make timber frames for the houses although 400 trees already felled still lay in the woods awaiting transport. By that year the first row of houses at right angles to the main street, still known as New Row, had been finished. It contained 26 houses which used local materials to construct oak or birch frames giving the town an English appearance. The houses were much like the half-timbered buildings which still survive in the English mid-lands. After this initial surge of enthusiasm problems began to appear. The absentee Irish Society grumbled at the cost and their worst fears were realised when two of their representatives who visited their new property confirmed that speculation was rife, especially among the society's own agents. By 1622 the number of houses in the town had grown to only 96 with 57 smaller thatched cabins. The town still had the appearance of a building site with the Diamond being described as filthy and problems with the maintenance of the walls were beginning to appear. By the 1630s more favourable reports began to filter back about the town, one visitor describing it as a 'splendid town'. Towns are not created overnight and over the next hundred years the society was to be well repaid for its admittedly heavy investment in the early years. By 1789 the society was clearing £2,335 sterling a year from its investment.

The seventeenth-century experience explains much of the subsequent history of Coleraine. Its enduring legacy was to be the street-plan and, at least until the nineteenth century, the fabric of the town. Visitors up to the 1850s could still see seventeenth-century houses in an irregular pattern around the Diamond and many commented that it looked untidy to the ordered eye of the nineteenth century. Indeed one late seventeenth-century house survived in New Row into the 1980s. Inevitably there were modifications to the street-plan over time to meet changing priorities but these were minor. Some of the early tenements proved to be too small and had to be amalgamated. The emphasis on defence, inevitable in the early years of the settlement and vital during the 1641 rising when Coleraine was besieged, declined over time. The wooden gates of the town were dismantled before 1710 and the ramparts fell into disuse and were built over, although even in the late eighteenth century they were enough of a landmark to be used as property boundaries.

If the most enduring legacy of the seventeenth century was the layout of the streets then probably the most influential one was the landlord. It was the Irish Society which helped to shape the character of the town through the eighteenth century. Politically they were absentees, leaving their agents to become involved in the often bitter urban politics of the corporation. The society helped to establish an infrastructure in the town. Initially this could be done through putting conditions into the leases made to their tenants. Usually such leases were for 31 years and there were general releasings of the town in 1660, 1692 and 1733. In the 1760s, however, they began to grant leases which contained provisions for renewal, in effect perpetuity grants, which meant that no new clauses could be inserted. The society then had to intervene more directly if it wished improvements made. In fact it had already been doing just that for a number of years. In 1742 it had funded the building of a market house, on the site of the present town hall in the Diamond, to the design of the London architect George Dance. Again in 1748 it paid for the building of a new bridge over the River Bann on the site of the present nineteenth-century structure which replaced an older bridge built in the 1670s.

Perhaps the most important project funded by the Irish Society was the construction of the quay at Coleraine. The original quay was constructed in 1611 and this was rebuilt in 1679, 1711 and 1739 and some other quays were also constructed privately. It was these quays which transformed Coleraine into a port and hence a bridge between its hinterland and the wider world. Despite the problems with the sand bar on the river it seems to have functioned well as a port from its earliest days with exports between 1612 and 1615 outstripping imports by nearly 50 per cent. By 1668 it ranked as the fourth largest port in Ulster. The cargoes which were shipped from these quays varied greatly over time. At some times in the eighteenth century it was people. In the 1760s two ships owned by the Galt family of Coleraine crossed the Atlantic eighteen times bringing 250 emigrants per ship on each trip to America. At other times in the century trade in the town was carried on in linen. Coleraine was an important centre for marketing the linen produced by local farmers. Cloth was woven locally and the pot-ashes used for bleaching were imported through the port of Coleraine. Local specialisms developed and by the middle of the eighteenth century fine linens 32 inches wide by 52 yards long became known as Coleraines. Two linen halls were built in the town to encourage the trade but were not used, merchants preferring the traditional market site of the Diamond where, according to one commentator in 1837, 1,000 webs could change hands in an hour on a Saturday morning. The linens were not usually exported directly, although in the nineteenth century some were to be. Most were sent through Belfast, Derry or Dublin. In return came the latest Dublin fashions. Tea, chocolate, pepper, aniseed and French barley were all available in the town in 1771. The shift in the linen trade to the Belfast factories in the early nineteenth century clearly shook Coleraine's economy. One unsuccessful attempt was made to introduce cotton spinning but the urban economy seems to have recovered to give the Victorian town its prosperous air.

Thus our story would seem to be complete: a street pattern which reveals a planned plantation town transformed into a Victorian provincial town by nineteenth-century rebuilding. However, there are still features in the Coleraine townscape which cannot be explained by this story. The first of these is the presence of a number of medieval castles near the town in the form of Anglo-Norman mottes. The oldest, at Mountsandel, was built in 1197, the second at Coleraine itself was constructed in 1214 and the third across the river at Killowen was put up in 1248. In themselves these might simply point to a defended crossing of the river, especially since we know there was a bridge there in 1241, if it were not for two other features. The parish church, dedicated to St Patrick, is referred to in 1337 and in 1351 Richard Fitzralph, the archbishop of Armagh, preached there. The existence of a medieval church on the present site is confirmed by the fact that the Irish Society did not build a church on that site in 1613 but repaired an older structure. A final indicator which suggests that the present settlement at Coleraine is much older than it looks is the street name 'Abbey Street', although this name is fairly recent. Between this street on the western edge of the plantation town and the river, workmen in the nineteenth century are reported as digging up human bones, stone coffins and remains of a stone structure. This is the site of a building shown on early seventeenth-century maps and it can only be the Dominican friary founded in the area in 1244, reorganised in 1484 and dissolved in 1534. Taken together the castles, church and friary all suggest that there was a medieval settlement on the site of the present Coleraine. Indeed this is probably the town mentioned in the ministers' accounts of Elizabeth de Burgh for 1353-60 which record the existence of a town and market, at which tolls were taken, in the manor of Coleraine.

We know almost nothing of this settlement except that it was a large one since the market tolls were the highest of all the de Burgh manors scattered over east Ulster. In common with most of the Anglo-Norman lordship it probably declined in the late fourteenth and fifteenth centuries leaving little except the castles, church and friary. The friary, together with a number of funeral monuments, was seen by the English lord deputy, the earl of Sussex, in 1556. During the sixteenth century the possibility of fortifying the site was considered a number of times. Indeed so important did the site appear that when a county was created in north-west Ulster in 1603 it was called Coleraine, the name only being changed to Londonderry after 1609 when the London companies became involved in the plantation scheme. Some attempt was made to create a town on the site of the present Coleraine by Sir Thomas Phillips, to whom the site had been granted after the rebellion of Hugh O'Neill. By 1607 Phillips had built 26 houses, which to judge from later maps were probably on the north side of Bridge Street. Perhaps when the Irish Society named their first street New Row it was to distinguish it from an Old Row made up of the remains of Phillip's abortive town.

The town of Coleraine is a reminder of the complexity of Ulster's past – Victorian in appearance, seventeenth-century in its design yet Anglo-Norman in its conception. It is also a reminder that the urban fabric must change with the times, sometimes with great speed. Coleraine is a town whose urban fabric is today changing at an unprecedented rate. In the 1960s alone its population increased by almost 40 per cent, evidenced by the growth of new housing estates around the historic core. The massive University of Ulster just outside the town recalls the changing functions of the settlement as does the new range of shops in the town, the architecture of some of which sits uneasily with their Victorian predecessors. Road-widening and the proliferation of car parks are some of the realities of the modern town but there is equally a need to ensure that what remains of the physical evidence of Coleraine's chequered past is conserved, despite the ravages of the developer and terrorist bomb.

Select bibliography

Coleraine Historical Society: *Ordnance Survey Memoir for the Parish of Coleraine, County Londonderry*, Coleraine, 1986
W. D. Girvan (ed.): *List of Historic Buildings ... in Coleraine and Portstewart*, Belfast, 1972
T. H. Mullin: *Coleraine in Bygone Centuries*, Belfast, 1976
T. H. Mullin: *Coleraine in Georgian Times*, Belfast, 1977
T. H. Mullin: *Coleraine in Modern Times*, Belfast, 1979

CARRICKMACROSS

Patrick J. Duffy

CARRICKMACROSS is located in the south of County Monaghan, on the edge of the great belt of drumlins that sweep from County Down to north Connacht, about 55 miles from Dublin on the main road to Derry. This frontier location in south Ulster, in the old barony of Farney in Monaghan, had an important bearing on the development of the town.

Carrick, as it has been called locally for more than two centuries, has a population of about 3,500 today. It is a town full of hustle and bustle, more than its small population would suggest. And this is an important aspect of Carrick's story: it is a town which caters for a busy and densely populated hinterland. This has been true for the past two centuries, not only for Carrick but for most of the towns of this region of small farms and dense population. In the last century, there were more than 400 persons for every square mile of land in much of County Monaghan: the old barony of Farney which was mostly served by Carrickmacross had more than 44,000 people in the 1840s. And towns like Carrickmacross in the past couple of centuries catered for the marketing, fair-day, drinking and rent-paying needs of the population. And emigration – one of the most thriving 'businesses' in these countrysides for 120 years – often began with an American letter from the town's post office and provisions for the journey from the town's stores. The two dozen pubs in the town today – more in the last century (one for every 100 people or so) – are not indicators of a town of heavy drinkers! They are, in fact, reflections of a town with a big rural population in its hinterland.

Most towns, like the rest of the landscape, have a story to tell. We all tend to highlight the unique aspects of the story. But the most important aspect of any place is the common theme; all our landscapes have developed through

Carrickmacross fair day c. 1900 (National Library of Ireland)

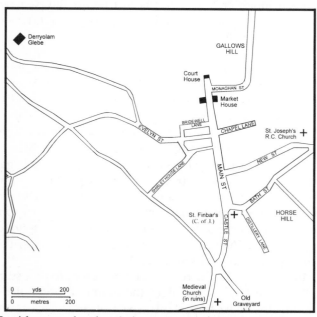

Carrickmacross, based on Ordnance Survey of Ireland, six inches to one mile, 1911

a common historical experience: the only differences are little local variations on the national theme – 'local rows', as Patrick Kavanagh from nearby Iniskeen said, were just expressions of broader national themes.

So what does this particular Irish town tell us? Because like most of our towns and countryside, the clues to its past are written in its landscape – it's just a matter of interpreting it. Carrick consists essentially of a long and wide main street on the long sloping top of a drumlin, closed at one end by St Finbar's Church of Ireland church and at the other end by the market house and the courthouse. These are some of the symbols of life and landscape in Irish towns up until probably the end of the last century. Off the main street are other reflections of the life story of Carrick: the Catholic church (originally St Mary's, now St Joseph's) located 'at the back of the town' (in the words of a petition to the landlord in 1780) at the end of Dawson Street (now O'Neill Street). The police barracks and jail were in Evelyn Street – called after one of the local landlords, Evelyn Philip Shirley. The Shirleys built a town house and rent office in Shirley House Lane. Behind the courthouse was Gallows Hill, where nobody was ever actually hanged, according to local tradition. The workhouse and the fever hospital were built before the famine to the north-west of the town on waste ground – well away from the good people of the town, though not far from the long and straggling terraces of thatched cabins which led off west along the Shercock road. Off the Dundalk road and along Bath Street, by contrast, Lord Bath in 1860 erected terraces of attractive cut-stone cottages, called Weymouth Cottages.

A different chapter in the story of the town is suggested by the presence of the old church ruins and graveyard at the bottom of the hill from Main Street in Magheross townland. Beside the graveyard was Tobar Inver or St Finbar's well. Less than a mile from the town on the Dundalk road is the little fishing lake of Lisanisk – Lios an uisce – where the MacMahons had their headquarters in the 1590s.

As in all small Irish towns, the past thirty years have seen an expanding girdle of new housing estates, making up what the census calls 'the environs' of Carrickmacross, which have recently outstripped in population terms the old town area.

Carrickmacross shares the experiences of a range of small Irish towns. Like many in the north, it began life as an identifiable town in the early years of the seventeenth century, in a part of Ireland where town life was a rarity: Gaelic Ulster was an exclusively rural domain. But by 1660, up to a hundred towns had become established in the province, each one the result of a combination of influences – landowner, merchant and crown.

The MacMahons who were the lords of Monaghan in the sixteenth century, like the other Gaelic lords to the north of them, showed no interest in town planning. Even Mac-Mahon's territory in south Monaghan was unlikely to afford the necessary conditions of political or economic stability for the establishment or growth of a true urban centre.

With the beginnings of Elizabethan English interest in the area, we have early records which help us to get a glimpse not only of the new developments and the newly-emerging landscape but also of what was there before: why, for example, was the site of Carrickmacross chosen? Did it have any pre-existing significance? We do know, for example, that in 1577 Richard Stanihurst of Dublin referred to Karreg Mack Rosse as 'one of the chief towns of Ulster'. So it certainly had significance – but Stanihurst's use of 'town' was probably a bit cavalier, and putting it at the top of the town league in Ulster was not saying much.

Monaghan was not included in the Ulster plantation, but it *was* surrounded by counties which were planted, and many of the new developments and new settlers in the neighbouring counties filtered into Monaghan. One of these developments was surely the idea of the town as a focus for settlement in the countryside. So Carrickmacross may be classified as such a plantation town, which grew up with the general goodwill but limited assistance of the local English landowner. Not that he was an insignificant personage. He was the third earl of Essex; his estate in Farney, which had been granted to his father Robert Devereaux in 1575, comprised more than 50,000 statute acres. Essex had a survey carried out in 1612 to establish the value of the estate and Carrickmacross is mentioned as a strategic location:

> There is no mill within the barony for which cause I think a mill would be very profitable and may be placed at Carrick Matherosse a very good market, kept on the Thursday and is situate directly in the middle of the barony.

This mill was one of the first developments in the new town. Next was the castle built by Essex *c.*1630. And in 1634, Thomas Raven, an experienced surveyor during the Ulster plantation, was commissioned to survey Essex's estate of Farney and he gives us the first early map of Carrickmacross which helps us look backwards at the significance of what existed before, as well as forward at the emerging shape of things to come.

The 1634 map of Carrickmacross shows a very simple structure. There are two elements in this picture of the emerging town. First there is the dominant castle of four storeys, with its bawn (or enclosed yard) – a typical plantation structure at the southern end of a straight street, with the market place clearly shown as a rectangular enclosure along the street. Also lining the street are several houses, with small enclosures running out behind them: the only substantial slated house was an inn – a pointer for the future! Another substantial house outside the town was the glebe house at Derryolam, which survives today. There were, however, long gaps on both sides of the street. Here was a town ready to be settled in, for those with the resources and nerve to start from scratch on this frontier of Ulster. The houses, drawn pictorially by the map-maker, are for the most part small thatched structures. Beside the castle and the street is a crudely drawn object which is probably the limestone outcrop which gave the town its name – *Carraig mhachaire rois* – quarried out for lime for agriculture by 1800. Indeed below the street and beside the mill dam is a lime kiln. And there is the mill, first proposed in 1612, with an extensive mill pond which continued well into the twentieth century as a significant feature of the town.

The most interesting part of Raven's map, however, is the large shapeless cluster of about forty thatched houses or cabins which can be seen grouped around the church and which stand in total contrast to the planned structure which was emerging up the hill. This is the church of Machaire Rois, founded by St Finbar in the seventh century, with its oval enclosure of trees (still extant today), holy well and wayside cross. Essex obviously therefore didn't pluck this site out of thin air: not many of the new towns of Ulster were true greenfield sites. Magheross clearly had some significance before. It is very likely that this is the Karreg Mack Rosse that Stanihurst referred to in 1577, and the place with the Thursday market in 1612 – a typical Gaelic settlement around the church, but hardly a town.

Though Raven's map shows what a pathetically small and underdeveloped place Carrickmacross was in 1634, it is a critical part of Carrick's story. It shows many parallels with new planter towns elsewhere: its smallness and lack of development are a reflection of the failure of plantation and settlement to set strong roots in this frontier land – not just because Essex was operating outside the official Ulster plantation, but also because it was too far south and too far from the heartland of the colonisation: Farney and south Monaghan remained a borderland of Ulster where settlers were thin on the ground and the town of Carrickmacross reflected this reality.

Small though it was, Carrickmacross was a focal point for attempts at settlement and development in Farney. When the rising broke out in 1641, a small group of settlers was trapped in the town, their names and their occupations showing a community huddling for safety in this vulnerable borderland. Robert Branthwait was in his chamber in the castle at eight o'clock in the morning when a group of men led by Pierce O'Birne hammered on his door. He took great offence – he being justice of the peace for the county and seneschal to Lord Essex. His servant Richard Fahy went out, they drew their weapons and Fahy pointed his pistol at them; then Branthwait, looking out of his window in desperation, saw Colla Mac Brian MacMahon (grandson of the famous Ever and a leader of the rising) riding round the back of the castle; he called to him and he was released. Small groups of settlers (some from Castleblayney) were imprisoned in the castle, the inn and glebehouse. Among them were Richard Cope from Armagh and Farney and Sir Henry Spotswood of Drumboat. In the massacre in January 1642, the following perished: Mr William Williams, his brother Gabriel Williams and brother-in-law Ithell Jones, who had the misfortune to be on a visit from Wales; Richard Hollis, manager of Mrs Usher's estate; John Morice, clerk to Sir Henry Spotswood; Rich Gates, just arrived from England as a clerk to Richard Blayney; Edward Crickley, receiver of Mr Dillon's rents; John Jackson, a tailor; Thomas Aldersey, a butcher in the town; and Thomas Trane, a Scotch peddler.

After the war the town recovered and lists of taxpayers provide us with fleeting glimpses of the town's borderland community. In the hearth tax returns of 1663 were names unfamiliar today – Thomas Davies, James Ramsbottom, Robert Williams, Thomas Kemp, Robert Hill, William Charity, Henry Marrall, Tobias Creefe, William Ragge, Thomas Higgs. Others listed were Owen Haughey, Patrick Haughey, Michael Gartlan, Owney McKenna, Hugh McAward, Hugh Duffy, Shane McIlmartin and Edmond O'Duffy, names that are still well known in the district.

The fate and shape of Carrickmacross, like most Irish towns into the eighteenth century, were largely influenced by the role of the local landowning class, which if it chose could have an increasing control of affairs in the town. The Essex estate was divided in two in 1646, coming through marriage to the Thynnes (lords Weymouth, later lords Bath) and the Shirleys (of Warwickshire). In this division the town of Carrickmacross was divided, with the boundary running down the middle of the main street.

It's hard to say how this affected the development of the town. Throughout the eighteenth century, for example, both Shirley and Bath were absentee landlords, though from 1750 Shirley built himself a house off the main street (recently demolished) which he used for short visits each year and which became the agent's house from the 1830s when Shirley built himself an extravagant mansion at Lough Fea to the south of the town. The lords Bath never resided in Monaghan, preferring the grander environment of Longleat in Wiltshire, where their descendants continue to live. Bath, however, established a reputation for interest in Carrick's affairs from an early stage. In 1711 he endowed a free school, which played an important part in the educational growth of the town for two centuries. Although it was clearly intended to assist the Protestant faith, from an early stage it catered for Protestant and Catholic and indeed there were Catholics on the teaching staff – a reflection of the borderland character of south Monaghan, outside the bastion of Ulster Protestant settlement.

Both Bath and Shirley frequently employed the same men as agents on their properties, which helped to maintain a balanced approach to the town's development. Maps of the estates in 1735 show essentially the modern layout of the Main Street, well filled out over the previous hundred years. There were about a hundred houses lining both sides of the street, with Carrick mill prominently located at the bottom of the hill on the Dublin road. The mill pond was marked as a lough and the infant market place noted in 1634 was now more formally marked by an arcaded market house in the middle of Castle Street and Main Street. And shops had begun to replace street stalls. After the famine, the two estates co-operated in building a new market house symmetrically laid out on opposite sides of the Main Street and an attractive feature of the town today.

By 1791, 54 new houses were built in Dawson Street, and as in most Irish towns, the Main Street layouts and facades were pretty well established by the middle of the last century: subsequent population decline and emigration froze further expansion for a hundred years till the growth of the 1960s.

Through the eighteenth and into the early nineteenth century Carrickmacross grew to become a busy country town, with a comparatively large Catholic merchant class, another reflection of its borderland situation. It had more than 2,900 people in 1831 and 560 houses (many of them squalid cabins); like many towns in Ireland it had thriving local industries, all due for setbacks following the union and the expanding market in factory-made goods from England. It had its own brewery and distillery employing hundreds of workers, seasonally and permanently: 200,000 gallons of whiskey were distilled annually!

A good sample of the economic diversity of life in Carrick at the beginning of the last century is provided by a list of occupations in the town in the 1820s:

Fourteen boot and shoe makers, based in Coote's Lane, Chapel Lane, Gallows Hill and Cross Roads;

Eight carpenters in Church Lane and Bath Street;

Eight blacksmiths in Bath Street and Penny Bridge;

Eight nail-makers, six saddlers; also rope makers, coopers, wheelwrights;

Ten bakers and five apothecaries – all on Main Street;

Five butchers – New Street and Penny Bridge;

Seven linen and woollen drapers;

Three dressmakers and milliners;

Two hat manufacturers

(Carrickmacross lace only really became established after the famine);

Six stone masons;

Eleven grocers;

Three earthenware dealers;

Three feather dealers;

Twenty-four spirit dealers – the biggest business of all, no doubt still selling Carrickmacross whiskey;

Three hotels, Commercial and Post Hotel and the Shirley Arms, on Main Street; and one in Bath Street.

The general market continued to be held on Thursday. It was especially good for pigs, which were sold to buyers from Dundalk, Newry and Belfast, and eggs, vast quantities of which were exported to Liverpool via Dundalk. The market also sold fresh and salt meat, salt herrings, fruit, salt, rosin, flax, meal, cottage furniture, frieze, haberdashery, nails, locks and hinges, heath and birch brooms and white bread.

The fairs on 27 May and 10 December were the biggest in the town.

In spite of this bustling situation, the army officer who wrote a report about the town for the Ordnance Survey in 1835 wasn't very impressed with Carrick. He particularly disapproved of the effects of fair days on the town:

> The houses in the main street are generally speaking large, but badly built and if examined are shells only, being run up as it were solely for the accommodation of hordes of country people who on all days, particularly Sundays and market days, frequent them for the purpose of drinking. The town is neither lighted, paved nor watched. The streets are tolerably clean, but during a market and the day succeeding it the pathways are a nuisance from the dirty habits of the country people, who seem to have little idea of delicacy.

The lower orders, he complained, were much addicted to dram drinking, many no doubt accustomed to merrily wending their way homewards into the hills of Magheracloone at Christmas time with candles stuck in their hat bands! Father Theobald Mathew and the temperance movement soon afterwards brought big changes to places like Carrick: no doubt the decline of the distillery was partly the result.

Before the famine, people moved around on foot, horseback or cart, carriage or coach, depending on their resources. For the poor from the town or hinterland, travel was limited and on foot; large numbers of labourers walked into the midlands and England to work the harvest each season. The better-off travelled by coach or horse car – using either the regular mail services through the town or cars for hire at the hotels: in the 1830s, the main coach from Derry passed through at 1 a.m., reaching Dublin at 7 a.m. The Monaghan day coach came through Carrick at 1.30 p.m., reaching Dublin at 7.00 p.m. It left Dublin at 8 a.m., passing Carrickmacross at 3 p.m. to arrive in Monaghan at 6 p.m. There were also Omagh coaches, Strabane coaches and mail cars to Dundalk, passing through Carrick at midday and 3 p.m. There were foot posts from the town to and from Kingscourt and Shercock daily.

Much of the rest of the nineteenth century saw a radical adjustment in the economic and social conditions of Carrick and Farney. The population had outstripped the economic resources of the region: the 1840s saw the erection of the workhouse which had nearly as big a population as the town's during the famine: in April 1851, when the census was taken, there were 1,700 people in the workhouse. Shirley tried to solve the looming crisis by paying the passages of many poorer tenants to America and Australia. During the 1840s up to 2,000 people were assisted with passage and provisions to the New World: all passed through Carrick, where many were kitted out and fitted with new clothes in the rent office, and ferried by hackney car or van to Newry, Dundalk or Dublin. In the 1850s, the Bath estate paid for the emigration of over 3,000 emigrants, of whom no record remains. Carrick's location of course made emigration fairly easy and thousands took the mail boat which plied daily from Dundalk to Liverpool. The coming of the railway to the town in 1860, connecting it with Dundalk, made the journey abroad even easier.

In the early part of this century, though the population of town and hinterland had fallen dramatically, Carrick still breathed through its weekly market, and William Daly's little journal is a finger on the pulse of the town during the War of Independence. A publican and member of the urban district council, he was very sensitive to the town's links with its surrounding countryside:

31 May 1921. Tuesday. Pork market opened £7.5 cwt. Weighing started 7 a.m. Train left 9.30 a.m. Order from police at the point of the revolver and gun all shops to close. Motors coming to town turned back and all people from the country ordered home. Police paraded the streets with their guns all day. Nothing done and when evening came two Black and Tans cleared the few stragglers off it at the point of their revolvers. Not a soul to be seen at 11 o'clock … 2 June. Thursday. Shops opened at 9 a.m. No people came into market. No business. Mary Courtney (barmaid) did not come in from 28 May (Saturday) as ambush was about a mile from her home where Perkins was shot. All schools were closed Tuesday and Wednesday and business was resumed on Thursday. Some of the Black and Tans ordered men and women off the footpath, clouted and kicked a good many of the boys, even one of the curates, Father Cullinan was ordered off and followed into the post office.

For much of the rest of the twentieth century up until the 1960s, Carrick's experience was similar to other towns of its size in Ireland – a declining or stagnating population and repeated attempts to encourage job opportunities for its population. Then through the 1960s and into the 1970s, the town's population has steadily grown with extensive new housing estates in the hills around it.

And the town of Carrick was also at the heart of the rhythm of life in the countryside. It was their window on the outside world, and Patrick Kavanagh was seeing it in this fashion when he included a reference to the magic of Carrick's fair day in a poem in memory of his mother:

And I see us meeting at the end of the town
On a fair day by accident, after
The bargains are all made and we can walk
Together through all the shops and stalls and markets
Free in the oriental streets of thought.

Select bibliography
E. P. Shirley: *Some Account of the Territory or Dominion of Farney*, London, 1845
E. P. Shirley: *The History of the County of Monaghan*, London, 1879
R. Whitehead: 'St Finbar's Church, Carrickmacross', *Macalla*, i (4) (1976)
P. Ó Casaide: 'Glenny's Houses', *Macalla*, ii (3) (1977)
T. McMahon: 'Some County Monaghan extracts from the 1821 census', *Clogher Record*, xiv (1991), pp. 92-114

TULLAMORE

Michael Byrne

A RECENTLY published guide for visitors to County Offaly had the curious title *Offaly: Undiscovered Country*. I like to think of Tullamore in the same way – as a town waiting to be discovered, a place full of surprises in terms of its history and its architectural remains.

The casual observer might consider the midlands as a largely rural society, without any significant urban base. On closer examination, the same observer might be surprised to see the extent of the towns of Portlaoise, Tullamore, Mullingar, Athlone and Longford. Athlone, of course, is the most significant with Mullingar and Tullamore in second and third place and Portlaoise and Longford the more peripheral.

Tullamore today has a population of 9,500 and is the county town in Offaly with a population twice the size of its nearest rival Birr. If Birr can claim to be the *Umbilicus Hiberniae* or navel of Ireland, and Roscommon, 'the heart of Ireland', then Tullamore must be 'the taste of Ireland'. The town is now famous throughout the world for its Tullamore Dew whiskey and Irish Mist liqueur. The whiskey is now made in Midleton, County Cork and the liqueur blended in Tullamore.

Tullamore occupies a central position in County Offaly and has been the capital town since 1833. The town is situated on the Tullamore River which divides it in half. To the north is the gravel ridge, the Eiscir Riada, known locally as the Ardan hills. To the south lie the Slieve Bloom mountains while to the east and west are flat boglands relieved only on the eastern side by the stump of an extinct volcano now known as Croghan Hill. The name Tullamore or Túlach Mhór, meaning the big mound or hill, probably refers to the hilly ground behind the junction of O'Moore Street and Cormac Street, once the location of the town's windmills. In the eighteenth century the town was also known as Tulla-

81

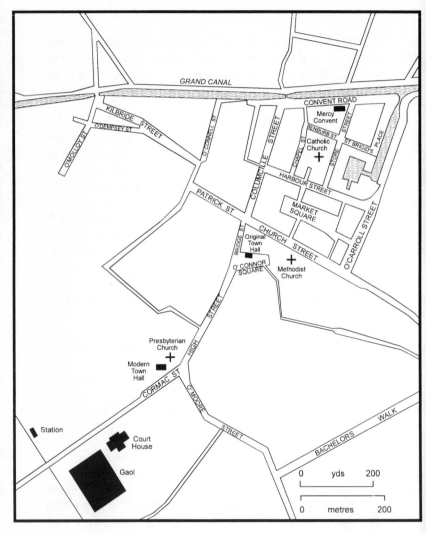

Tullamore, based on Ordnance Survey of Ireland, six inches to one mile,
1912

Old Canal Hotel, Tullamore, demolished 1974
(photograph property of Michael Byrne)

moore', a name introduced by former owners of the town, the Moore family.

Tullamore lies in the ancient district of *Fear Ceall* which has been translated as 'men of the woods' or 'men of the churches'. Neither would be inaccurate because Fear Ceall was once covered by vast bogs and forests. The area was famous for its monastic centres at Clonmacnoise, Durrow, Lynally, Clareen and Birr. The route to Clonmacnoise was across the Esker while the Durrow to Birr monasteries were on a north-south corridor through the bogs. If holy places such as Durrow and Clonmacnoise were once significant population centres, nothing now survives save the monastic remains. What is of interest is the way in which the old monastic north-south corridor continues to impact on the modern road transport system. Much of Tullamore's traffic comes from the Mullingar-Athlone routes heading towards Portlaoise and Birr. The east-west traffic by-passes Tullamore at Kilbeggan seven miles north of the town. The most leisurely way to arrive in Tullamore is by canal or rail.

Coming by canal boat will present an image of a holy place with the town's principal churches in view. The Catholic church, somewhat secluded in the back streets of the town centre, has a substantial spire to identify its location. This church was erected in 1802, and demolished and rebuilt in 1902. It was destroyed by fire in 1983 and again rebuilt at a cost of over three million pounds. The new church has an impressive timber interior and some Harry Clarke Studio windows. St Catherine's, the Church of Ireland church designed by Francis Johnston and opened in 1815, is placed prominently on a hill to the south-east of the town. Arriving by rail, the first sight to greet the visitor will be the former Gothic-style county jail of 1826, and beside it, a substantial neo-classical courthouse of 1835 – the latter still in use and the former now divided into small industrial units. Either way, the visitor cannot escape civil and religious authority. A brisk walk through the main streets will reinforce the feeling of authority and of some taste because the town is laid out on a grid-iron pattern with the principal street running from the Kilbeggan road canal bridge to the north and the Birr road railway bridge to the south and beyond it Charleville Castle, the home of the former owners of the town, the earls of Charleville. This castle, designed by Francis Johnston, is considered one of the finest Gothic-style country houses in Ireland and is now open to the public. Work on the castle began in 1810 and was completed in 1812.

The oldest house in Tullamore is another castle, a tower-house known as Sragh Castle observable from the railway line and dating to 1588. Nearby was the original O'Molloy castle, shown on early maps and mentioned in the grant of the district to the Moore family in 1620 in the course of the Stuart plantations. The grant to John Moore of some 20,000 acres, in so far as it related to Tullamore may have been a formality, because Moore had already acquired the lands through a series of mortgages raised by the O'Molloys. John Moore was the son of Thomas Moore, an Elizabethan soldier, who had received lands at Croghan Hill in east Offaly in the

1570s as part of the first Offaly plantation. The Moore family let on long lease their Tullamore lands throughout the seventeenth century, choosing to reside at Croghan Castle instead.

There are no accounts available of Tullamore in the seventeenth century. We know it had a castle, a watermill and a few cottages in the 1620s. The fact that the landlords were not resident in the town in the seventeenth century would have hindered development. Surviving tax collection data of 1660 would suggest that the Tullamore town population was not much more than 100 and in rank order well below Birr, with a population of over 700. Birr was settled by the Parsons family (later earls of Rosse) in the 1620s and by 1641 was seeking county town status from Daingean or Philipstown, with a population of some 250. Daingean was the county capital, more by historical accident than design. As the location of an English fort inside enemy lines from the 1540s, it acquired county-town status in the emerging new county of Offaly (or King's County as it was known until 1920), under an act of Queen Mary in 1557, which laid the basis for the Laois-Offaly plantation.

It was not until after 1700 that Tullamore developed as the town we know today. In the population stakes, it outstripped Birr only in the second half of the nineteenth century, but had already defeated Daingean by the 1720s. Viscount Molesworth, Daingean's landlord, writing in 1724 from his town to his wife a letter of complaint regarding his urinary tract infection, said, 'I am in a place where no herb or drug that I might have occasion for, can be had nearer than Tullamore'. The Moore family moved from their home at Croghan Castle in the early 1700s and built a large house in the vicinity of the present Tullamore harbour. No trace of this house now remains. Through political influence, they were able to secure a barrack to house a hundred foot soldiers in 1716 (at the same time as that in Castlecomer) and by the late 1720s, a Protestant church was built in what is now Church Street, then known as Church Lane; nothing now remains of this building. The demise of Daingean's county-town status, which did not come about until 1833, was signalled as early as 1767 in a special county infirmaries (amendment) act, passed to facilitate the establishing of the Donegal county infirmary at Lifford rather than Letterkenny, and that for Offaly at Tullamore in place of Daingean.

Evidence of industry and house-building in Tullamore is available from landlord estate records, the Registry of Deeds and from what survives on the ground and in the street-names. The building of the barrack provided an impetus to business. Entrepreneurial immigrants, such as Huguenots from their settlement at Portarlington and Quakers from Mountmellick and Edenderry, turn up as lessees in the building leases granted by the landlord. The first recorded building lease is one for John Moore to Richard Brennan, in 1713. His premises are now the Brewery Tap in High Street. Part of what is now O'Connor Square was known as the Market Place or New Street in the 1740s.

Notwithstanding the by-passing of Tullamore by the main trade routes to the south (via Daingean and Birr) and the west (via Kilbeggan and Moate), it continued to grow in the first half of the eighteenth century. Landlord influence was obviously a factor but so were structural forces such as the need to create a market centre east of the isolated Garrycastle barony which comprises much of west Offaly, and west of Daingean surrounded as it was by bog. One geographer has remarked that towns are the essential cog in the machinery of rural society. Tullamore's chief economic function would have been as a market centre for the predominantly rural population. The principal trading days were those on which markets and fairs took place. Captain Thomas Johnston, the lessee of Charleville demesne in the 1760s to the mid-1780s, wrote in March 1765, 'I am a stout farmer, between four and five hundred sheep, fifty calves, besides cows and horses, and I want two hundred sheep more as soon as the rents come in'. At the time, pasturage was still predominant in Offaly with tillage of much less importance.

Although tillage was less significant, it played a major part in the economy of towns such as Tullamore. The Tullamore distilling business, dependent as it was on oats and barley, developed rapidly in the 1780s and survived until the

1950s. Agricultural activity reflected itself in trade with the woollen and tanning industries important. So also was the linen industry. In 1754 Charles Moore, now earl of Charleville, gave a lease for a factory building for the linen business. These premises were in lower Church Street but do not now survive except in the name Pike's Lane – Pike being a linen weaver. In fact by the 1780s Offaly was a leading county for the manufacture of linen outside of Ulster.

By the mid-1760s Tullamore would have consisted of Patrick Street, Church Street upper, Bridge Street, part of O'Connor Square and some development in High Street. Town development received a set-back in the 1760s following the death of Charles Moore, first earl of Charleville. He had removed himself from the town of Tullamore to Charleville Demesne in 1740. He had encouraged building development through the provision of cheap sites on the basis of an annual ground rent of a shilling a foot in front with the lease for lives renewable for ever. The procedure was that the tenant nominated three lives, usually young healthy people, and when the three people died the landlord would accept three new lives at a nominal fine so far as town houses were concerned. For town parks the rent could increase substantially. This was the basis of all building in Tullamore until the advent of freehold sales in the 1920s. It provided a cheap site while the landlord enjoyed on-going revenue and a measure of control of the building development at commencement stage and later by means of covenants in the leases.

On Charles Moore's death the property passed first to his sister's husband, John Bury of Shannongrove, County Limerick, who died soon after in a bathing accident at Ringsend, Dublin. The Tullamore property, together with Limerick and Dublin estates, then passed to Moore's nephew, Charles William Bury, an infant of six months. During the Bury minority there were no leases of more than 21 years granted and thus no new building activity.

Charles William Bury's coming of age in 1785 coincided with the famous balloon fire in Tullamore. The fire was caused by an air balloon catching fire in what was only the third attempt to make such an ascent in Ireland. This led to the destruction of about a hundred houses in the Patrick Street area. The fire had caused no damage in the Bridge Street, High Street, O'Connor Square area of which Arthur Young may have been speaking when he recorded in 1776 that part of Tullamore was well built. Nevertheless, John Wesley in his journal for 1787 felt obliged to remark: 'I once more visited my old friends at Tullamore. Have all the balloons in Europe done so much good as can counter-balance the harm which one of them did here a year or two ago?' Wesley's view that most of the town was burnt down was repeated by Charles Coote in his Offaly survey for the Dublin Society, published in 1801. Coote looked at Tulla-more as a very neat town which owed its newly acquired consequence to the present Lord Charleville. 'About fourteen years ago it was,' said Coote, 'but a neat village, with scarce any better than thatched cabins, which were almost all destroyed by accidental fire ...' The Coote and Wesley comments are only partly true because many of the fine houses in Bridge Street, O'Connor Square and High Street pre-date the fire, as does the Williams head office in Patrick Street.

Charles William Bury, the first earl of Charleville (of the second creation), presided over the fortunes of Tullamore from his coming of age in 1785 to his death fifty years later. The burning of Patrick Street gave him an opportunity to let the properties there on new leases and widen the street in the process. During this time the population expanded three-fold to over 6,000 in 1841. The new streets, such as Offaly Street, Harbour Street and William Street, all followed the grid-iron pattern and a second market square was provided in the 1820s. The Tullamore tenants petitioned the Irish house of commons in 1784 and in 1786 to designate Tulla-more as the county town in place of Daingean, but because of the significant political influence of the Ponsonby family, now owners of Daingean, this was not achieved until 1833. The county jail was built in Tullamore in 1826 and the coun-ty courthouse in 1835. The landlord went to considerable trouble about the design of his Gothic-style jail by the Pain brothers and the neo-classical courthouse by J. B. Keane.

Lord Charleville did not develop the residential or commercial properties himself save the town hotel, which is still in use. Instead Charleville brought in the middlemen to build and sell or retain, either way at a profit rent. Chief among the developers or building speculators was Thomas Acres. His 1786 house is now the headquarters of Tullamore urban district council. Acres and his family were involved in the building of some 140 houses in the town, or some 15 per cent of the housing stock in the 1900s. There were other speculators too and between them the town as we know it (excluding the centre core which is pre-1785 and suburbia which emerged after 1900) was completed between 1785 and the eve of the famine in 1845. All the older buildings of note in Tullamore were erected at this time, including:

1) Charleville Castle, erected between 1800 and 1812.

2) St Catherine's church – Church of Ireland dating from 1815 – with its Bachelor's Walk which was designed to give the landlord access to the church from his castle while avoiding the town.

3) The old Catholic church, erected in 1802.

4) The former town hall in O'Connor Square, erected in 1789.

5) The county infirmary in Church Street, erected in 1788 and now lying derelict.

6) The county jail of 1826 – now Kilcruttin Centre for small industries and prior to that Salts (Ireland) Limited spinning mill.

7) The courthouse of 1835 by J. B. Keane, architect. This was destroyed by the republicans leaving the town in July 1922. It was rebuilt and continues to serve as a courthouse but is largely laid out as offices for Offaly county council.

8) The Mercy convent, erected in 1838-1840, demolished and rebuilt in the mid 1960s.

9) The workhouse, erected in 1841 at Ardan Road and demolished in the 1970s, brought to an end the public building programme.

Landlord influence facilitates supply more than being a determinant of demand. The general upturn in the Irish economy after 1785, which continued until the recession after the ending of the Napoleonic wars in 1815, was a spur to development. So also was the improvement in transport when the Grand Canal was linked to Tullamore in 1798 and to the Shannon in 1804. The canal passenger traffic led to the building of a new hotel in 1801 which, after the end of passenger traffic with the advent of the railways, served as a parochial house until its demolition in 1974. The goods traffic must have been enormous because stores were built near the new harbour in what is now Store Street (these stores were destroyed by fire about 1960). The canal boats provided a direct link with Dublin at low cost facilitating the transport of turf, bricks, grain for malting and Tullamore limestone from the local quarries.

While the town turned its back on the river flowing through its centre and surrounded it with mills and industrial buildings, the canal at the northern end is open and an important visual amenity now serving as a linear park and a line to the Shannon for pleasure craft. The canal marked the northern boundary of the town until the 1900s, as did the railway line from 1858 on the southern side. Some of the poor of the town lived on the northern bank of the canal near the convenient water supply and beside the bog of Puttaghan. It was this area which suffered most during the famine years. The remaining poor lived in lanes at the back of the big private houses fronting the streets, and paid rents of sixpence or a shilling per week with the 'lease' determinable every Friday. At that time, and until the development of Charleville Road (the road to the landlord's demesne) after 1900, status was not so much having a house in a particular part of town as having it fronting the street.

The post-famine years, and up to the end of the First World War, saw the steady consolidation of Tullamore's position as the leading town in Offaly. Whereas the population of Tullamore and Birr was virtually the same, at 6,300, in 1841, by 1926 the population of Birr had fallen to almost half that figure, and that of Tullamore to about 5,000. In fact,

Clara because of the Goodbody jute business was the only town in Offaly to experience growth in the period 1861 to 1926. The towns had not fared badly by contrast with the rural areas and the county as a whole. The population of Offaly in 1841 was almost 147,000, falling to 53,000 in 1926. It has been stuck in the 50,000s ever since and in the 1991 census was 58,494, down 1,400 on the 1986 figure.

The Charleville influence declined after the 1840s and the earldom was extinguished with the death of the fifth earl in 1874. The merchants and the farmers came to prominence through the advent of public boards such as the board of guardians of the Tullamore poor law union (established after 1838), and the Tullamore town commissioners (established in 1860, so as to facilitate the provision of a town gas supply). The commercial role of Tullamore expanded after 1890, with the development of the general merchant business of P. and H. Egan and D. E. Williams. Akin to Liptons and Findlaters, both firms had a system of branch shops throughout the midlands, connected to an agricultural food processing base in malting, brewing and distilling. The Goodbody tobacco factory provided significant employment until a fire destroyed the factory in 1886 and the entire workforce was transferred to new premises near Harold's Cross, Dublin. The Tullamore distillery business expanded in the 1870s and again after 1900 when D. E. Williams developed the Tullamore Dew brand. The distillery closed in 1954 with the brand name sold in the 1960s and surviving stocks by the 1970s.

The main sources of employment up to the 1930s were in malting, distilling, stone quarrying and distribution. In the mid-1930s, Salts (Ireland) Limited established a spinning mill in the old jail which, behind protective tariffs until the mid-1960s, provided employment to upwards of 1,000. This factory closed in 1982 and jobs for men in Tullamore have been in short supply since. Foreign industries backed by the Industrial Development Authority such as Burlington (now Atlantic Mills), Sherwood Medical, Lowe-Alpine and Snickers between them provide about 800 jobs, and most of these are for women. The Midland Health Board and Offaly county council employ about 600. The current unemployment figure for the Tullamore district is 2,100, comprising some 1,500 males and 600 females. Shops and services are a significant source of employment for the town. Although Tullamore has no more than 15 per cent of the county's population, it has 50 per cent of the business and draws from a hinterland of at least 30,000. The town is now poised for further expansion with the construction of the Bridge Centre at Bridge Street which will provide a new road system, over 300 car parking spaces, 44 residential units and 80,000 square feet of shopping space. Housing after 1900 saw the clearing of the town lanes and the building of over 1,500 houses by the urban council in the suburbs. Private sector development in the suburbs commenced on Charleville Road after 1900 and got going in earnest after the Second World War. There is now a strong demand for town houses, curiously enough, in the very lanes where the 'cabin suburbs' were once situated.

Tullamore has managed to preserve much of its original townscape. The major public buildings are well presented, especially in the town square. The emphasis on timber shopfronts with painted lettering is having an effect. Shopping facilities have developed to the extent that the trip to Dublin is not a must. The town is served with three local newspapers and local radio. All sports facilities, including a tartan track, but excepting an indoor swimming pool, are available. All that is lacking are more job opportunities.

Is there a *deus ex machina* in town growth? I like to think not. No one influence, from landlord to government to structural economic forces, is primary. Growth is a complex organic process. Writing of Georgian London, Sir John Summerson remarked that 'a town, like a plant or an anthill, is a product of collective unconscious will, and only to a very small extent of formulated intention'. Tullamore, I believe, well fulfils that viewpoint.

Select bibliography

T. W. Freeman: 'Tullamore and its environs, County Offaly', *Irish Geography*, i (5) (1948), pp. 133-50

M. Girouard: 'Charleville Forest', *Country Life*, 27 September 1962, pp. 710-14

M. Byrne: *A Walk through Tullamore*, Tullamore, 1980

W. Garner: *Tullamore Architectural Heritage*, Dublin, 1980

M. Byrne: *Tullamore Town Album*, Tullamore, 1988

Tullamore Urban District Council: *Tullamore Official Guide*, Sligo, 1993

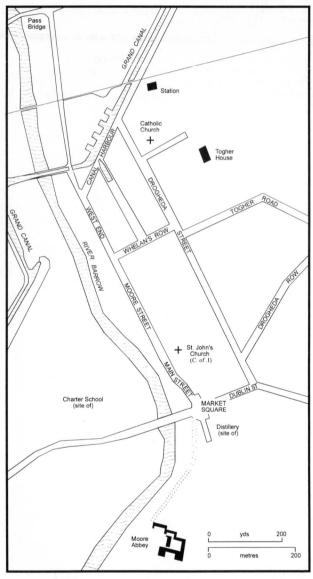

*Monasterevan, based on Ordnance Survey of Ireland, six inches to one
mile, 1939*

MONASTEREVAN

Arnold Horner

FOR some readers the mention of Monasterevan may evoke memories of the 1975 siege involving the kidnapped Dr Tiede Herrema, or associations with Count John McCormack and the nineteenth-century poet Gerard Manly Hopkins. However, this County Kildare town is probably most likely to be recognised as one of those places that must be negotiated on the route between Dublin and the south and south-west. Going from Dublin, the eighteenth-century road from Kildare town runs straight across an extensive, now much-altered, bog. It makes a line toward a turreted, now closed, entrance to Moore Abbey, the demesne and big house that lies to the south of the town. Then the road veers north and west to skirt the demesne wall and briefly cuts through the town between the tall, austere, buildings of the former distillery. The intersection with the town is quite brief, and the traveller may scarcely notice that this route has also cut between the main gates of Moore Abbey to the south, and a small market square to the north. Almost certainly there will be no time to notice the monument in the market square commemorating Father Edward Prendergast and the bloody skirmish that took place there in 1798. For the traveller, it is usually quickly on, across the Barrow bridge and into County Laois.

But this kind of brief encounter misses much about this unusual town. Most of Monasterevan actually lies along two straight, parallel, streets that each extend for about 600 metres north from the main road. Train travellers, as they push rapidly across the Barrow railway bridge, catch a good glimpse of one of these streets and a clear view of the prominent tower of St John's Church of Ireland church. Both streets in fact extend as far as the Grand Canal, the Athy branch of which crosses the Barrow at the north end of Monasterevan. The canal is now little used but it, the adja-

Moore Abbey and Monasterevan from the south in 1933
(Photo: Aerofilm)

cent and now unroofed canal company stores, and the unusual aqueduct that takes the canal across the Barrow, make a remarkably tranquil, elegant, contrast to the discordant urgency of the aggressive long-distance travellers at the south end of the town.

To appreciate this town further we could perhaps start by looking at a large-scale map. That map shows immediately that the main street is mostly lined by buildings on one side only. Those houses seen by the train traveller are faced on the far side of the main street by their own front gardens extending down to the River Barrow. Only at the south end of the main street, near the market square, is this pattern broken. Here we have buildings on both sides, the main street narrows, and its straight alignment is lost as the street swings slightly eastward to enter the square.

Looking further across the map, we may see that the second principal street, Drogheda Street, is also only partly lined by buildings. If the map is of recent date, we will also notice an extensive scatter of low-density housing to the east and south-east of the main town. Much of this housing was built by Kildare county council at a period when councils preferred greenfield sites to the more difficult challenge of renewal and infill. The result is that very few of those travellers hurrying past Monasterevan today will have realised how remarkably extensive the town has become for its population of just over 2,000.

But I want to explore the overall impression our large-scale map offers of the town plan. Notwithstanding new building and some other small-scale changes, the street layout of the main town is basically the same as it was 150 years ago. As early as the 1830s, the six-inches-to-one-mile Ordnance Survey map shows a street layout that, like that of today, is slightly irregular at the Moore Abbey end but has as its main feature the two wide, straight, parallel streets leading to the canal. Our overall impression is of a *planned* layout, the sort of rectilinear arrangement that we find repeated in many places across Ireland, from large cities like Dublin and Limerick to smaller places like Gorey, Cookstown and Mitchelstown.

For anyone interested in urban history, that layout poses many questions about when, and by whom, the development was created. It arouses our curiosity about what Monasterevan looked like in earlier centuries. Was it laid out like this from the time of its foundation, or was there some major redevelopment of an earlier layout? Exploring these questions further is our focus.

For many Irish towns, answering such questions can be quite frustrating. Pre-nineteenth-century town records are frequently patchy affairs that make the jigsaw of an urban history difficult to assemble. In the case of Monasterevan, the town is particularly fortunate that the critical late eighteenth-century period can be explored in some detail.

A combination of three major types of historical sources

– maps, property deeds, and estate records – will provide our information. Maps made of Monasterevan in 1762, 1773, 1807 and 1833 display the changing layout in considerable detail, and would at any time be of value for the urban historian. In the case of Monasterevan their value is further enhanced because so many records of contemporary property transactions also survive. For the period between 1700 and 1820 about 200 memorials of Monasterevan property deals are preserved in the Registry of Deeds in Dublin. There are a further 50 deeds, leases and other documents about Monasterevan before 1800 in the tin boxes in the National Library of Ireland containing records from the estate of the earls of Drogheda. Allied to the periodic base data of the maps, these documents help fill in much of our re-planning puzzle.

Before going further, however, it is necessary to set our scene by reviewing those aspects of the earlier development of Monasterevan that help us understand its shape and growth. Right up to the 1600s, really very little can be said about Monasterevan as a village. Its very early history involved the founding, on the ancient route of the Slí Dhála and near a ford across the River Barrow, of a seventh-century monastery by St Evin. Later, probably about the year 1189, the Cistercians established the monastery of Rosglas. This monastery probably occupied the site of the present Moore Abbey, and was of sufficient importance to send representatives to the Irish parliament. But its location left it increasingly insecure, beyond the Pale and in an unstable countryside. After the dissolution of the monasteries in 1536, part of the abbey was turned into a fortified manor house.

From the seventeenth century onward, more definite information is available about the actual village. A grant for a Saturday market was issued in 1614. Some forty years later, a population count of 1659 showed Monasterevan as being about the same size as nearby Rathangan but much smaller than neighbouring Kildare town or than the other County Kildare towns of Naas, Athy, Maynooth and Castledermot. From early eighteenth-century property leases, we begin to get some sense of places and people within the town. There are references to the market place and market house, to the tanyard, to the corn and malt mills, to a tuck mill, and to two saddlers and a dyer. There was probably also an inn.

In the 1730s, Monasterevan gained more of that staple of so many small towns, the passing trade. A new turnpike road was built to facilitate long-distance traffic. The old road from Kildare town had skirted the bog and crossed the River Barrow at the Pass Bridge just north of the village. In contrast the new road ran straight across the bog and through what is now demesne land to enter the village near to the present Moore Abbey house. It then headed northwards along the village street before turning sharp west to cross the Barrow by a bridge which is now gone but which was located opposite the present St John's church.

By the 1730s, too, the ownership of Monasterevan had passed into the family who were to be the proprietors throughout the town's late eighteenth- and nineteenth-century development. The Moore family, the earls of Drogheda, had already been involved in a major early eighteenth-century development initiative on Dublin's northside, but in Monasterevan, their initial involvement was undramatic. An attempt was made during the 1750s to expand the local economy by establishing a short-lived linen industry. Otherwise, the main initiative was to support the building, in the 1750s on the west bank of the River Barrow, of a nursery to raise small orphans as hard-working Protestants. This large building later became a charter school, which closed in 1828. Its original purpose long abandoned, and now known as the 'Hulk' and much the worse for wear, this structure remains a prominent feature just to the north of the modern main road.

The new spirit of landlord-inspired improvement already evident in some other mid-eighteenth-century Irish towns did not really become manifest in Monasterevan until the 1760s. By then, Charles Moore, the sixth earl and later first marquess of Drogheda, had taken over. As far-reaching changes took place during his 64 years as landlord, we are fortunate that one of his early acts was to commission a survey of his estates. Bernard Scalé's huge map of 1762 is of great interest because it shows old Monasterevan as quite different to the planned town on the later Ordnance Survey.

Scalé's map shows the village as a single winding street of variable width, with the big house of Moore Abbey, the Protestant church and the mill all very close to its southern end. The main part of the village stretched over several hundred metres as far as the bridge. In this area were the inn, the market house and most of the better dwelling houses. Further north, after the bridge turn, there was a broken line of cabins and beyond, more isolated, the tanyard, the school-house, the 'common' and the old Pass Bridge. In total, there were around 100 houses and cabins, suggesting a population of around 500 or 600. Significantly, the map shows no place of Catholic worship. An early eighteenth-century mass house was at Coolatogher, a mile and a half north of the village. Later, the Catholic chapel was sited near the Pass Bridge, at the farthest extreme from the big house.

Shortly after Bernard Scalé made this survey, Charles Moore began his improvements. These took place in three major stages. The early changes, made in the mid-1760s, were improvements to the earl's own immediate property. Moore Abbey was extensively renovated and – in keeping with contemporary fashion – attention was also given to the remodelling of the surrounding demesne, with a small extension and minor road closure being made on the east side.

Not long afterwards, the Protestant church was re-sited to a prominent location almost opposite the bridge. The map of 1773 shows the new church in this position, with its gates set back from the existing street. Its tower is virtually in line to close the vista for travellers moving eastbound along the long straight turnpike road from Queen's County. Here was a new landmark, expressing the prevailing religious domination and also foreshadowing the new street layout.

But these projects were only the beginning. Further northward extensions of the demesne could only be achieved by pushing the village itself further north. Yet such a process was attempted during the 1770s and early 1780s to such an extent that ultimately at least a dozen dwellings were removed from the south end of the village. At the same time the area north of the new church, which had formerly been occupied by the tanyard and about eleven cabins, was cleared and laid out as a new street. By 1780, development was sufficient for the description 'new street or road' to be included in a lease granted to a John Murray.

Without outside stimulus and outside investment, further changes might have taken place only slowly, and would probably have remained quite small-scale. But a new, third stage of improvement was precipitated by the arrival of the Grand Canal in 1785. Monasterevan was now on the Athy branch of the canal, which would link to Carlow and Waterford via the Barrow Navigation. As a director of the canal company, the earl of Drogheda might already have been anticipating the possibility of a branch from Monasterevan westward into the midlands, indeed maybe something more substantial than that made four decades later, the 11-mile branch to the other Drogheda estate town of Mountmellick.

At any rate, the argument could now be advanced that Monasterevan was well-positioned and that an early stake at a good site in the new canal town might give investors a good return. Indeed this argument appears to have been used to such effect that Monasterevan became the focus of a mini-speculative boom in the mid 1780s. Between 1785 and 1788, a series of building leases were issued for sites in the general vicinity of the canal, and these attracted the attention of some Dublin and Carlow merchants, as well as receiving the approval and cash of some of the canal engineers. Such was the strength of speculation that it proved possible to impose rigorous building conditions. The stiff penalties for non-compliance would have been the envy of a modern planning office. For example in 1787, Thomas Coldclough, of Dublin and King's County, was bound 'in the penal sum of £800' that he would:

> within one year ... build two good substantial dwelling houses of lime and stone two storeys high and covered with slates and eighty-four feet in front finished in a good workmanlike manner according to a plan designed by Colonel Tarrant with a paved footway with a hammered stone band in the front thereof six feet wide in Drogheda Street in Monasterevan.

Colonel Charles Tarrant was one of the canal engineers, and had also been associated with the wide streets commission in Dublin. In another 1787 lease there is a reference to the building of a two-storey house 'in front and elevation at least equal to the plan given by Colonel Tarrant'. From these comments it looks as if he had an important role in planning what was by 1789 being referred to as the 'New Town of Monasterevan'.

A mixture of speculation, confidence and ambition thus characterised the first years of the canal. Indeed, ambition reached such heights that at some heady moment Monasterevan was being visualised as a major inland canal port, with a new unprecedented scale of development. We know this because a carefully-drawn plan of such a major development was superimposed, and can still be traced, on Bernard Scalé's map of 1762. It shows a radically re-aligned road from Dublin, a re-positioned market house, a new bridge and an extensive rectilinear street plan. Four new streets would run parallel to the existing main street, with a series of cross-streets and lanes. But perhaps the most striking feature of this remarkable plan is a new arterial canal running parallel to a new main street as far as a new market house, and then veering sharply east to create a major new east-west axis. At least in the mind of this plan's designer, the canal was quite literally central to the future of Monasterevan.

Much of this plan never came to fruition. Some very elegant buildings were erected at the canal end of the town, most notably the well-proportioned terrace of seven three-storey Georgian houses that now make up Monasterevan's West End. They stand comparison with the best Georgian architecture in any Irish town. New projects did continue into the early nineteenth century, the most significant being the canal aqueduct of 1826 and the development around 1832 of a new bridge and new section of road to allow the turnpike route to take the line it still follows and continue straight across the market square. For this scheme, the old, free-standing, market house in the middle of the square was removed. The map of the town made in 1833 shows these changes, and effectively shows the town as it appeared at the end of the landlord phase of redevelopment. By then over 80 new houses had been built in the development area between the new church and the canal, and the effect of improvement was clearly evident in the 1841 census statistics. Monasterevan was then a town of almost 1,100 people, and three-quarters of its 150 houses were categorised as first or second class houses. In contrast, less than a quarter of the houses were so classified at the nearby town of Kildare, where there had been no attempt at rebuilding.

Yet measured against the blueprint imposed on Scalé's map, the Monasterevan of the 1830s might be regarded as an under-achievement. Of the blueprint street plan, only the line of Drogheda Street and a small canal-end section of a third street had actually been laid out by the 1830s. Of the canal plan, only a small, now filled-in, canal branch was actually developed. The push to expand had really run out of momentum quite quickly. The reasons for this are various. Monasterevan itself was quite small and could only support limited new development. Returns from the canal could not immediately match the expectations of the early speculators. The bloody events of 1798 highlighted hitherto suppressed instabilities. The landlord now spent most of his time in London.

In the long run, however, the future well-being of Monasterevan turned as much on another individual's enterprise as upon its landlord's improvements. Monasterevan Distillery was founded, probably near the site of an earlier brewery and distillery, by John Cassidy in 1784. This flourished throughout the nineteenth century and sustained the town over a period when many other centres experienced population loss. The map of 1807 shows Cassidy's commercial interests already extending to both sides of the turnpike road. Their growing power was emphasised when the Cassidy family acquired Monasterevan House, the most elaborate of the late eighteenth-century houses on the main street.

The emergence of the Cassidys has the added significance of highlighting a shift in the religious balance of Monasterevan. The peripheral position of the eighteenth-century mass house contrasts with the centrality of the established church and surely symbolises how the contemporary landlord viewed the two denominations. But the supply of Protestant tenants was insufficient to sustain any major new development. The economic power of the Cassidys marks the reality that the Catholic population were crucial to the future of nineteenth-century Monasterevan. Tangible expression of their new status came with the building of the elegant church of Saint Peter and Paul about 1847. Significantly, this was on land held by Robert Cassidy at the canal end of the town. It was into this general area that the Christian Brothers moved in the 1860s and where the Mercy Sisters came in 1898. With the building of schools and a presbytery, and perhaps also James Cassidy's building of Togher House, a Victorian-style big house, a new centre of power can be said to have emerged to counterbalance the landlord at the far end of the town.

These shifts within the town were taking place at the same time as much wider social and economic changes within Ireland. The building of the Dublin to Cork railway during the 1840s had particular long-term significance, for it limited the potential of the canal and ultimately of the town also. It is true that some trade continued on the canal until 1960 and that Monasterevan also had a railway station until that time. But the ultimate significance of the railway, and to an even greater degree of twentieth-century road communications, was to facilitate centralisation and the development of a relatively widely-spaced network of medium-sized and large towns. Monasterevan found itself with only a minor role in this development, and has remained primarily, as it has always been, a local service centre for the surrounding countryside.

As many other small towns have discovered, such a role does not necessarily mean irreversible decline or stagnation. The 1920s and 1930s were a low period in Monasterevan's history, with the failure of the distillery and the departure of the landlord. But the old mainstays have been replaced by new sources of vitality – to such extent that over the last fifty years the population has doubled. The big house, Moore

Abbey, will soon have been for fifty years a Sisters of Charity home for mentally handicapped girls. A precision engineering works was established on the distillery site during the 1930s. More recently other industries have been established, most notably a couple of knitwear firms, one of which employed a labour force of over 200 in the early 1970s. Local activities have provided valuable employment over the years, but many Monasterevan people also commute to work or study in surrounding towns and indeed Dublin. That there is confidence in the future is evident from the significant volume of private building which has been added to 200-plus local authority houses built in recent decades.

Monasterevan today is a fascinating mix of well over 300 years of urban development. The medieval monastic phase is well concealed within Moore Abbey, but the seventeenth and early eighteenth centuries are exposed in the outline of the market square and in nearby sections of Main Street. Elsewhere, the regular street-plan incompletely flanked by late eighteenth-century building is a last testimony to the high hopes of the age of improvement and early canal era, while the main Dublin-Cork road is still flanked by tall nineteenth-century industrial buildings. In between are many other buildings I have not had time to mention, the early nineteenth-century Methodist meeting house for example. To really appreciate this town, with its distinguished and varied heritage, you must get out of your car, give yourself time, and walk. You should not be disappointed.

Select bibliography
Countess of Drogheda: *The Family of Moore*, Dublin, 1906
E. Ryan: *Monasterevan Parish, County Kildare: Some Historical Notes*, Naas, 1958
J. Holmes: 'Monasterevan distillery', *Journal of the County Kildare Archaeological Society*, xiv (4) (1969), pp. 480-7
M. Quane: 'Monasterevan charter school', *Journal of the County Kildare Archaeological Society*, xv (2) (1972), pp. 101-21
A. Horner: 'A mid-eighteenth century scheme for a County Kildare linen industry', *Journal of the County Kildare Archaeological Society*, xvi (4) (1983-4), pp. 317-28
G. Carville: *Monasterevan: Valley of the Roses*, Monasterevan, 1989

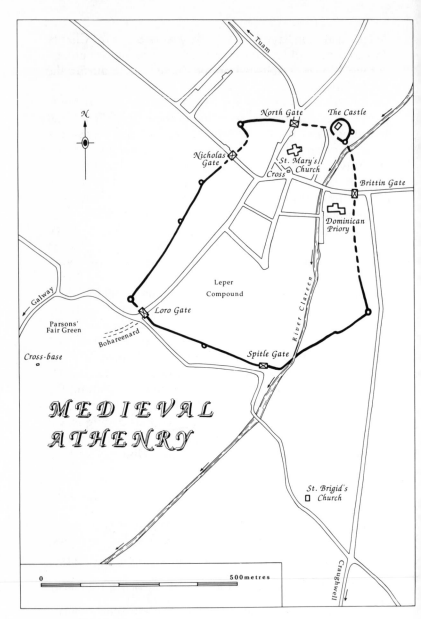

Medieval Sites in Athenry, by Etienne Rynne

ATHENRY

Etienne Rynne

ATHENRY, fifteen miles east of Galway city, has a past that goes back several millennia. Quite apart from polished stone axeheads from the general area, other prehistoric objects found locally include a fine late bronze age spear-head and bronze shield, and the bronze chape from an early iron age Celtic sword-scabbard. The region also featured prominently in Early Christian Irish history, notably nearby Tysaxon (Tech Sachsan, the Saxon's house) where Balan, who came to Ireland with Colman after the synod of Whitby in A.D. 664, founded a monastery.

The region no doubt played an important role in early history, the river ford which gives Athenry (*Baile Átha an Ríogh*) its name clearly being significant: it is where the east-west route along the Esker Riada, across the narrowest part of Ireland, crosses the most westerly possible direct south-north route. It played a similar role in much more recent times when Athenry became the main east-west – north-south junction on the railway network. However, it is only with the coming of the Anglo-Normans in the late twelfth century that medieval Athenry began to exist, at least in theory – in 1178 the title baron of Athenry was created for Piers de Bermingham, making it the premier barony of Ireland, well before 1235 when Richard de Burgh, lord of Connacht, granted a charter to Meiler de Bermingham, second baron of Athenry, who founded the actual town.

Meiler de Bermingham built a fine strong castle over-looking and guarding the river ford. He also instituted an adjoining strongly defended town, which included a large parish church, a central meeting-place (the market square), and a few short years later a fine Dominican priory. That the ford was important to the Irish too is perhaps to be seen by what is probably the earliest historical reference to the town, namely the attack by the O'Connors in 1249 – when the Irish

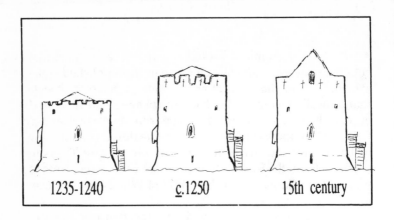

Athenry castle, three phases of building, with reconstructed view of c.
1235 by Etienne Rynne

were decisively beaten, fleeing at the sight of Norman
cavalry. A holy well known as Lady Well, just over half a

mile to the south-east of the town, is believed to have associations with this battle and is still a major site of pilgrimage on 15 August each year.

Due, no doubt, to its strategically important siting medieval Athenry had an eventful history. It was raided many times by the Irish and in August 1316 was the scene of a major battle between the newcomers under William de Burgh and Richard de Bermingham, and the Irish, under Felim O'Connor, king of Connacht. Victory went to the townspeople, a result which so severely affected Edward Bruce's Irish campaign that it changed the course of Irish history. In the 1570s the sons of the earl of Clanricarde attacked Athenry 'and so damaged the town that it was not easy to repair it for a long time after them', according to the *Annals of the Four Masters*. The lord deputy Henry Sidney began repairs about 1576 when, apparently, it was decided to reduce the town in size by about a half: a map dated 1583 shows this dividing wall, but as less than half finished, despite which for all practical purposes the present residential area within the walls is still more or less confined to the northern half of the town. The Clanricardes attacked again in 1577, 'setting the new gate on fire ... and driving off masons from working on the wall'. In 1597 Athenry was again sacked and this time so severely destroyed by Red Hugh O'Donnell that it never really recovered; the town became fossilised, with the result that Athenry today is *the* classic Irish medieval town.

Athenry still retains not only its medieval castle, parish church, Dominican priory, market cross, and typically medieval street plan, all within its medieval town walls, but also the base of a bargaining-cross in the fair green, two medieval bridges across its river, the Clareen, the remnants of a pre-reformation church dedicated to St Brigid, and a working forge, all immediately outside the town walls; there is also a uniquely triangular-in-plan dovecote within the town, but this is post-medieval (eighteenth century) in date. The five major medieval monuments within the town, however, are of sufficient importance to deserve individual description – after all, they are what make Athenry an outstanding Irish heritage town.

For almost five centuries Athenry castle has been abandoned, roofless and in a ruinous state. In 1990, however, the national monuments branch of the office of public works started work on its restoration. The restored castle will be used, among other things, as a heritage centre to explain the town and immediate vicinity to interested visitors and scholars. The reconstruction has just recently been completed and now resembles something approaching its appearance shortly before its abandonment in the fifteenth or sixteenth century when the de Berminghams are said to have moved into a more comfortable dwelling in the town square.

Athenry castle consists of a keep and surrounding curtain-wall or bawn. The original keep, built about 1235 by Meiler de Bermingham, was low and squat, the roof being at the level of the present second floor. Shortly afterwards, probably by Piers, Meiler's son who succeeded him in 1252, the castle was raised in height by another storey; in the fifteenth century the gable-ends were raised to accommodate a new and higher roof rising above the battlements.

Entrance to the castle was by external wooden stairs leading to a decorated doorway in the east wall at first-floor level. Two narrow but fine windows remain at this level, both decoratively carved like the doorway; such carved work is unique to Athenry castle though quite common in ecclesiastical buildings of the late twelfth-early thirteenth centuries. Also unique to Athenry castle is that over its doorway was a small stone-built canopy-like affair, presumably to provide some shelter for visitors at the door.

The castle seems to have generally been cold and dark: there are no windows at second-floor level and no fireplaces anywhere; the fire was probably centrally placed in the uppermost room at whatever period of construction, the smoke escaping through a louvre or opening in the centre of the roof. It is no wonder the de Berminghams moved eventually from it to a more comfortable town house in the square.

The town walls of Athenry are easily the finest medieval town walls surviving in Ireland. They enclosed an area of about 28 hectares (69 acres), thus putting medieval Athenry into the top group of Irish walled towns regarding size. Until 1979, when eight monstrous, shiny grain-silos were erected immediately to the south of the town, Athenry was the only place in these islands where medieval town walls could be viewed as they were intended to be viewed, that is across open fields with the town snugly ensconced behind.

While the original town defences probably consisted of an earthen rampart with outer fosse or moat, and a wooden palisade on top, a three-year murage grant was obtained in 1310 and the walls, for the most part, date from that period. There is a tradition, recorded by the Galway historian James Hardiman in 1820, that the walls of Athenry were built out of profits gained from the sale of arms and armour taken from the fallen after the battle of Athenry in 1316, but this is clearly fantasy. The threat occasioned by the battle, however, probably did give rise to a strengthening of the walls, perhaps by the addition of the towers which are not bonded into the wall and thus may be later, secondary additions.

Built of mortared stone, the walls are thin, averaging about 1.1 metres (just under 3 ^{1}/2 feet) in thickness. The presence of an 8-metre (26 foot) wide, flat-bottomed, originally water-filled moat outside the walls adds to their height when seen from the outside. They averaged about 4.5 metres (14 ^{3}/4 feet) in height originally, but this includes an outer breastwork or parapet on the top which thus created a wall-walk whereby defenders could move around the walls, defending the town from vantage-points other than the wall-towers and town gates.

The finest of the surviving wall-towers is that at the north-eastern corner of the town. It is 10.1 metres (almost 33 feet) high and, like the others, was built with a solid base. It had two entrances, one from the top of each adjoining wall, so that the defenders could pass through the tower as they patrolled around the town walls. Within the tower is a short stairway leading to a partitioned room which had three internally-splayed windows allowing those within to survey the outer faces of both adjoining walls and also the area straight out from the tower itself. The other towers were all no doubt basically similar.

Though the map of 1583 shows only four gates into the town, one in the west wall, two in the south wall, and one in the east wall, it seems unlikely that there would not have also been one through the north wall, judging from the present street plan which seems to be the same as that originally laid out in medieval times. However, the only surviving gate in Athenry today is right there: the North Gate, or 'The Arch' as it is more popularly known. It has some architectural features which would suggest that it might indeed be of late date, including evidence for a thick and heavy portcullis and a 'murder hole', which is strategically placed to allow defenders to hurl stones or spears down at attackers under the arch attempting to destroy or lift the portcullis.

On the 1583 map the four other gates are named: 'Nicholas Gate' through the west wall, 'Loro Gate' and 'Spitle Gate' through the south wall, and 'Brittin Gate' through the east wall. Loro Gate, nowadays called 'Swan Gate' after a public house which is thought to have stood nearby during the last century or two, opened on to the old road to Galway. Spitle Gate clearly gets its name from a hospital which must have been within that part of the town, where it would have been well away from the inhabited part of Athenry thus segregating the sick from the populace in an effort to avoid the spread of contagious diseases. Why Nicholas Gate was so called is not known, but Brittin Gate got its name from that of the owner of the land there in the mid-thirteenth century, Sir Robert Braynach, his name deriving from *Breathnach*, a Briton or Welshman.

The de Berminghams built a parish church for themselves and their followers, soon after their arrival. By the late fifteenth century the church required considerable repairs, and in 1484 Archbishop Donat O'Murray of Tuam suppressed the rectory and vicarage and made the church collegiate with a small community of eight secular priests and a warden. Ninety years later it was destroyed by the earl of Clanricarde's sons, even though the mother of one of them is said to have been buried there!

A sturdy, cylindrical column of thirteenth to fourteenth-century type can be seen embedded in the south wall of the nave, while the remains of tracery in the northern transept and the sculptured corbel and piscina in the southern transept indicate a fifteenth-century date for them. From this one can deduce that the original thirteenth-century parish church was a wide rectangular structure consisting of an aisled nave and chancel, and that when the church became collegiate its aisles were demolished, the arches separating them from the nave blocked up, and the two transepts added, thus giving it a cruciform plan.

In 1828 a small rectangular church, with a particularly elegant spire at its western end, was built by the Church of Ireland in the chancel. This remained in use until 1967, and for the past few years has served as a scouts' den, but now is being renovated for use as a Heritage Centre.

Normally, in Ireland, Dominican priories were built just outside the town walls, but not in Athenry, though this might be explained by its being sited on the other side of the river from the rest of the town, even if just within the walled area. In 1241 Meiler de Bermingham, founder of the town, presented the site to the Dominican friars so that they might build an abbey – reputedly at the request of St Dominic himself; the saint, however, had died in 1221, twenty years earlier. Strangely enough, both the native Irish and colonising Anglo-Normans co-operated in sponsoring the construction, and the priory was completed in 1261. In 1324 the front of the church was knocked down and rebuilt with a fine traceried window and, no doubt, a fine west doorway, the former now partly and the latter totally destroyed by a handball alley built into it about the turn of the present century. The choir was lengthened and a north aisle and transept were added about the same time.

In 1400 Pope Boniface IX granted a bull of indulgence to those who visited the priory and who contributed alms towards its upkeep. In 1423 the priory was accidentally burnt, and Pope Martin V granted another bull of indulgence to those who contributed to its repair, an indulgence which was renewed in 1445 by Pope Eugenius. Alterations made during the lengthy period of rebuilding included reduction of the size of the fine east window, replacing its ornamental cusped tracery by the more severe switch-line variety, and the heightening of the roof of the cloistral ambulatory. The major change, however, was the construction of a large central tower, which necessitated strengthening the aisle's columns and reducing its arches – despite which it fell in 1845. Under the tower was erected a roodscreen, of which there are only three other examples in Ireland.

The priory escaped suppression in the dissolution of Henry VIII, but in 1574 Queen Elizabeth gave the friary buildings and lands to the provost and burgesses of Athenry for all of 26s 6d (£1.32^1/$_2$) yearly. In 1627 Charles I granted the priory to four Galway merchants to hold it for the king. These merchants were, however, well disposed towards the friars and the Dominicans were therefore able to re-establish themselves in Athenry in 1638. There followed a brief period of restoration work, the sacristy and perhaps the hagioscope, popularly misinterpreted as a 'leper squint' or 'penitent's cell', apparently being additions dating from then. In 1644, due to favourable conditions resulting from the confederation of Kilkenny, the priory of Athenry was erected into a university for the Dominican order by decree of a general order held in Rome. Disaster befell the monastery in 1652 when Cromwellian soldiers wrecked the buildings, and in 1698 the priory was formally closed by the penal laws.

In the mid-eighteenth century the cloistral buildings were demolished and a barracks built there for a regiment of English soldiers who are recorded as having broken or defaced nearly all the tombs and other carved stones in the priory. In 1819 the soldiers were replaced by the police militia, which later became the Royal Irish Constabulary, who were later transferred to a new barracks built for them in Cross Street. In 1892 the Priory of Saints Peter and Paul was taken into state care as national monument number 164.

The Dominican priory is noted not only for its varied history and architectural remains, but also for one of the finest and most interesting collections of medieval grave slabs in rural Ireland; it also contains some fine wall-plaques and two important and imposing tombs.

114

In Athenry's square is an unusual monument consisting of a steeply stepped pyramidal base on which is set a carved socket-stone with an upright, rectangular sculpted stone in its top. Though known as the Market Cross, this monument does not really present the appearance of being a cross, despite the carving of a crucifixion on one face of the upright stone. It is, however, the last remnants of a fine late medieval Gothic cross of 'tabernacle' or 'lantern' type. Such crosses, dating from the fifteenth century, are well known in Britain and elsewhere in Gothic Europe, but for Ireland the Athenry monument is a unique example. These crosses get their name because instead of a transom as a cross-head they have a rectangular swelling, which has an appearance vaguely resembling a lantern or tabernacle. Almost invariably such crosses have a plain, tapering, shaft set into a sculpted socket which is on top of a large and often quite high stepped pyramidal base. The Athenry market cross fits into this general pattern, except that the long shaft is now missing.

On the top of the stepped base is a virtually square block, the original socket-stone for the now-missing shaft. It is carved with, among other things, two opposed jani (mythological quadrupeds with single horns which they could swivel around to face their enemies); these latter resemble those on the doorway into Clontuskert abbey, near Ballinasloe, which is dated to 1471 and which thus helps date the Athenry cross. With its now-missing shaft, the total height of the cross would have been something in the region of 5 metres (16 feet) – a truly impressive monument indeed. The Athenry market cross is, furthermore, the only market cross of any type in Ireland which still stands in its original position.

The purpose of market crosses is two-fold, primarily to give the town a central focal point and secondarily to serve as a place where bargains struck at the market would be sealed. Although the market cross in Athenry is clearly of late fifteenth-century date there can be little doubt that it must have had predecessors, probably of wood. Historically we know little about the Athenry market except that in 1629 permission to hold a regular market in the town, and a fair in October, was granted to Sir William Parsons, whose name is still applied to the fair green, with the base-stone of its bargaining cross, just outside the town to the south-east, close to the former town gate leading to Galway.

And what about Athenry today and in the future? There are plenty of good things going for Athenry, but also some which are less than fortunate – bad, in fact. The good includes the fact that the townspeople are at long last beginning to appreciate their past and the medieval monuments which make the town unique. This good, however, is counteracted by some thoughtless and unfortunate recent buildings which lessen the value of this medieval inheritance. Chief among these is the cluster of eight unsightly metal grain-silos erected in 1979 almost slap up against one of the finest stretches of the town walls; these now present visitors approaching the town from the Dublin and Limerick directions with a truly unwelcoming and ugly sight.

The Kenny Memorial Park, one of the better GAA grounds in the west of Ireland and for many years the training centre of County Galway's highly successful hurling teams, should certainly be classed as 'a good thing' for Athenry, but it also offends – by the grandstand built not so long ago almost back-to-back with the town wall, the roof of which remains obstinately visible from the outside.

Another real plus for Athenry is 'Westrail', a locally based group which organises steam-train excursions between Galway and Athenry during the summer months. They have persuaded Iarnród Éireann to repaint the railway station in a darkish green, thus bringing it back to something more closely resembling its past. But once again all this is somewhat spoilt by the removal of the slated roof of a fine mid-nineteenth-century stone-built goods-transference building.

Nor did the closure of the station as one of Ireland's main railway junctions in 1976 help: no longer can one travel by rail from the west northwards to Claremorris and Sligo, nor southwards to Ennis and Limerick, without first travelling across the Shannon – ridiculous! Athenry by its very siting is a natural junction between east-west and north-south, and, as already mentioned, was always regarded as such, the town owing its very existence to that fact. Indeed, it was the arrival of the railway there in the mid-nineteenth century which started the town's revival and gave it a real chance to regain something of its former status.

The railway bridges between Athenry and Galway were clearly built to take two lines of tracks, though whether the second line was ever laid or was laid and later lifted, is unknown to me. Either way, its absence has undoubtedly proven the greatest handicap to Athenry's growth: it removes any realistic chance Athenry had of becoming a really viable commuter town for Galway. But while there's life there's hope, and Athenry is looking ahead with optimism to the future.

Before finishing, a word or two about the town's name. The name of the town is an Irish one, *Baile Átha an Ríogh*, which indicates that the ford must have been of importance in pre-Norman times. As no kings are known to have ever had any connection with the region at any time, the name should be translated as 'the town of the river's ford' rather than as 'the town of the king's ford' as it generally is. *Rige* is an ancient Indo-European word for a river; many rivers are called the Rye, including one joining the Liffey at Leixlip, and others in Yorkshire and the Isle of Wight – indeed, the River Rhine may likewise have derived its name from the same term. This may, furthermore, explain the present-day pronunciation of the town's name: it would surely be 'Athenree' were kings involved.

Yes indeed, kings or no kings, the town has had a great past and can confidently look forward to a great future. As an archaeologist I'm glad I chose to live in Athenry.

Select bibliography

S. Lewis: *A Topographical Dictionary of Ireland*, London, 1837, i, pp. 82-4

H. T. Knox: 'The Bermingham family and Athenry', *Journal of the Galway Archaeological and Historical Society*, x (1917-18), pp. 139-55

H. T. Knox and M. Redington: 'Notes on the *burgus* of Athenry', *Journal of the Galway Archaeological and Historical Society*, xi (1920-21), pp. 1-26

C. McNeill: 'Remarks on the walls and church of Athenry', *Journal of the Galway Archaeological and Historical Society*, xi (1920-21), pp. 132-41

A. Thomas: *The Walled Towns of Ireland*, Dublin, 1992, ii, pp. 8-13

TUAM

Paul Gosling

ACCORDING to a story current amongst the school children of Tuam in the late 1980s, the town once featured as a question in the popular TV series, *Mastermind*. 'What is the smallest city in the British Isles?' asked that doyen of quizmasters, Magnus Magnusson. What the contestant's reply was, is unclear, but the word 'Pass' is probably not far off the mark. However, at the end of his question-time he must have been surprised, as indeed the school children were, to learn that the answer was 'Tuam'. Obviously, some explanation was necessary, and was forthcoming with the quizmaster's qualification that Tuam was an ecclesiastical city!

Such recognition, while welcome, deserves scrutiny. Much of the early history of Tuam does indeed revolve around ecclesiastical affairs. Until its amalgamation with Killala and Achonry in 1839, it was the see of the Protestant diocese of Tuam, and it is still the cathedral town of the Catholic diocese of the same name. Thus, this modest town contains no less than two nineteenth-century cathedrals as well as large portions of their medieval and Romanesque predecessors. These and other remains bear testimony to an ecclesiastical lineage which extends back almost 1,500 years to the early sixth century A.D. when Jarlath founded the first monastery there.

Little of historical substance is known of St Jarlath, apart from some colourful moral tales which inform us that he performed 300 genuflections every day and night! However, most authorities agree that he lived in the late fifth and early sixth centuries, and his family appears to have belonged to a branch of the Conmaicne tribe who inhabited part of north Galway and south Mayo. Tradition holds that having been educated by St Benignus at the Patrician monastery of Kilbennan, two and a half miles north-west of Tuam, he

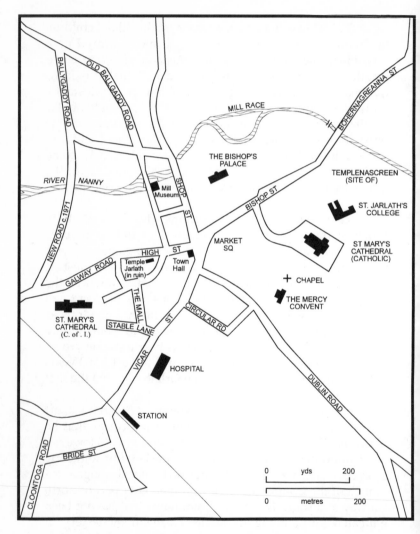

Tuam, based on Ordnance Survey of Ireland, six inches to one mile

120

founded a monastic school at Cloonfush, two miles west of the modern town. The reason for his eventual removal to Tuam is explained in a delightful piece of hagiology which records a prophecy of St Brendan of Clonfert. When he was a pupil at Cloonfush, St Brendan foretold that St Jarlath would not die there but at the spot where the wheel of his chariot would break. In order to fulfil this, the aged Jarlath mounts his chariot and leaves Cloonfush. The wheel duly breaks at Tuam where he founds a church and later dies.

The location which fate chose for Jarlath's monastery was a fortuitous one, situated, as it was, close to a crossing point on the River Nanny, a tributary of the River Clare. Though flanked to the north-west and south-east by extensive bogs at Halfstraddle and Curraghcreen, the site itself was located on a low ridge. At this point, the River Nanny actually flows through a narrow cut in the ridge, possibly an old glacial channel, the sides of which are still up to six metres in height. Though now largely obscured by the cluttered buildings in the centre of Tuam, these landscape features serve to explain the full name of the town. In Irish, this is rendered as Tuaim Dá Gualainn which translates as 'the ridge (or mound) of the two shoulders'. Much speculation has surrounded the existence and identification of the possible 'mound' referred to in the name, and unsubstantiated traditions of the existence of a tumulus behind the new library building, in Shop Street, are current locally. However, on present evidence, the most likely solution is that 'tuam' here refers to the natural ridge, and the two shoulders to the steep sides of the cut on either side of the old ford on the River Nanny. This was situated beside the present Mill Museum, and the profiles of the two 'shoulders' are still reflected in the relatively steep slopes of Chapel Lane to the south of it, and Old Ballygaddy Road to the north.

On a wider horizon, the spot chosen by St Jarlath for his monastery was also strategic, in that it was located on one of the important routeways from the midlands through the then extensive bogs, turloughs and riverlands of north Galway. To the west, it gave access to Cong, and beyond it, via the narrow pass between Loughs Corrib and Mask, into

121

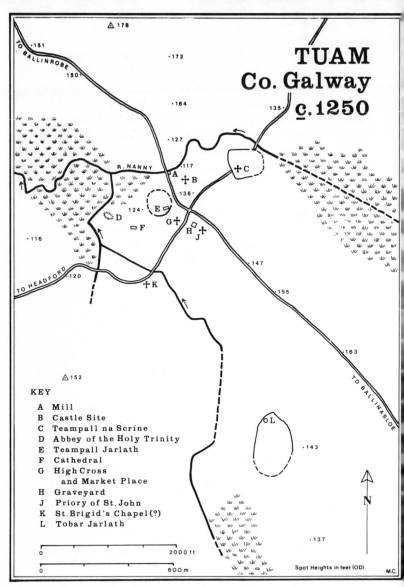

KEY

A Mill
B Castle Site
C Teampall na Scrine
D Abbey of the Holy Trinity
E Teampall Jarlath
F Cathedral
G High Cross
    and Market Place
H Graveyard
J Priory of St. John
K St.Brigid's Chapel(?)
L Tobar Jarlath

0   2000 ft

0   600 m

Spot Heights in feet (OD)

Tuam, archaeological sites by Paul Gosling

west Connacht.

Apart from the obits of a few abbots at 'Tuam-da-ghualainn' mentioned in the annals, nothing is known of the early history of St Jarlath's monastery. Even its exact site is far from clear, though attention has tended to focus on Temple Jarlath. This ruined thirteenth-century church stands in the old pre-reformation graveyard on the west side of High Street in the modern town centre. Leo Swan, whose research has contributed so much to our understanding of the appearance and layout of early monasteries, has pin-pointed this site as the focal point of St Jarlath's monastery.

Swan's work has identified the presence of large oval or circular enclosures around many of our early monastic sites. Though now often fossilised into modern field or property boundaries, their presence indicates the original extent of these monasteries. Within their limits would have been located the church and graveyard of the monastery, along with the scriptorium, guesthouse, farm buildings, work-shops, the dwellings of the monks and possibly some tillage plots and gardens. At Temple Jarlath, the curving eastern and southern boundary wall of the graveyard almost cer-tainly mirrors the line of one of these sub-circular enclosures, in this case about 120 metres in diameter, which once sur-rounded the church.

However, within a mile of Temple Jarlath there are the sites of two other early churches not considered by Swan, both of which are also encircled by large sub-circular en-closures. The first, now situated in Bishop Street, less than 400 metres to the north-east, is known as Templenascreen, the church of the shrine. Though no visible trace of it now survives, this church is referred to a number of times in medieval sources. According to one late version of the *Life of St Jarlath*, it owes its name to the fact that it once contained 'a precious shrine' containing the saint's ashes and his other holy relics. The existence of this shrine is in fact attested as early as 1135 when the *Annals of Loch Cé* record that the 'Cathach of St Iarlaithe [was] laid waste by the Dalcassians'. What has survived, however, is the line of most of the circumference of the monastic enclosure, about 110 metres in diameter, which originally surrounded this church. Today, this is preserved in the modern property and townland boundaries on both sides of Bishop Street particularly in the curving line of an old laneway to the north of the street. Before the widening of Bishop Street in the early eighteenth century, this lane probably carried the main road from Tuam towards the north-east, to Dunmore and beyond.

The third early church site lies in the townland of Toberjarlath, on the southern outskirts of the town, just over half a mile south-east of Temple Jarlath. Here on the verge of the railway line, just north of the railway bridge on the Athenry road, is the site of St Jarlath's Well. Though the well itself was removed during the construction of the railway in the 1850s, a small plaque now marks this hallowed spot. This well stands in the northern part of the largest of Tuam's three early ecclesiastical enclosures. Oval in plan, and over 175 metres in diameter from east to west, over half of its circumference is preserved in townland and field boundaries. And though the interior is now flat farmland, there is a vague local tradition of a church here.

Which, if any, of these three large enclosures marks the site of St Jarlath's early monastery is an open question which only archaeological excavation can answer. At any rate, they are likely to represent a sequence of development stretching from the foundation of the monastery, in the sixth century, to its *floruit* in the twelfth. Their very presence also indicates the extent of the early monastery, suggesting that by the twelfth century it had a number of settlement foci. In this, Tuam bears comparison with some of Ireland's other major monastic sites, like Clonmacnoise, Louth and Armagh, which also possess multiple foci, each marked by one or more churches.

In the twelfth century, historical sources document the rise of Tuam from relative monastic obscurity to national prominence as a major ecclesiastical centre. The vehicle for Tuam's spectacular precipitation onto the historical map was the church reform movement, the most lasting legacy of which was the introduction of a diocesan system of organisation into the Irish church. At the synod of Rathbreasil in 1111, Tuam was designated as one of 26 new diocesan sees in Ireland. Its choice as the administrative centre of a new diocese, one of five in Connacht, was undoubtedly due to the influence of the O'Connors, the most powerful dynastic family in the west at this period. The family appear to have established one of their chief residences at Tuam in 1049 after Aedh O'Connor defeated the O'Flahertys for possession of this part of north Galway. Tuam's subsequent history was to be closely tied to the rising fortunes of the O'Connor family who held the kingship of Connacht from the later tenth century onwards. In fact, in the persons of Toirdelbach Ó Conchubair (1088-1156) and his son Ruardí (1156-1197), the family dominated the political map of Ireland for most of the twelfth century. Thus, the elevation of Tuam to archiepiscopal status at the synod of Kells in 1152 was no surprise. This synod set Tuam alongside Dublin, Armagh and Cashel as one of four 'metropolitan' sees in Ireland, each at the head of its own ecclesiastical province.

The surviving architectural remains reflect Tuam's rise as a major ecclesiastical centre. In the course of the century from c.1120 to 1220, the physical face of the monastic settlement appears to have been transformed by a number of bold architectural and artistic projects, most of which were executed under the patronage of the O'Connors. Thus, we can note the erection of four high crosses, the construction of a 'castle' and a cathedral, as well as the foundation of two new monastic houses. However, one of the earliest indications of Turlough O'Connor's espousal of Tuam as a major ecclesiastical centre is the beautiful metalwork cross, now known as the Cross of Cong, which he commissioned. This was crafted sometime between 1119 and 1136 as a processional cross for the monastery at Tuam. Designed to contain a fragment of the true cross, its presence must have greatly enhanced the monastery's status as a pilgrimage centre, by then already widely known for the cult and cures surrounding the relics of St Jarlath.

The foundation c.1140, of the priory of St John the Evangelist, brought with it the stricter observance of a European monastic order, probably Augustinian. Its adoption was undoubtedly the result of the first waves of the church reform movement then beginning to affect Ireland. St John's priory was located in the Circular Road area and though not a stone of its fabric now survives, part of its site was still occupied by a graveyard in the mid-nineteenth century. Furthermore, the head of one of the high crosses was found near here in 1926.

In 1161, the *Annals* record the erection of a 'castellum' at Tuam. Whether it was the design, or the novel use of stone in its construction, which inspired this description is unclear. No definite traces of it now survive, though the enigmatic feature known as the 'the Chair of Tuam' is pointed out as part of the castle. This diminutive semi-circular stone-and-mortar structure is embedded in a boundary wall immediately north of the present Market Square. However, the Ordnance Survey letters, compiled in 1839, record that the castle 'stood across the centre of Shop Street' which would place it slightly further to the west. In either case, the site was a good one, on the crest of the slope overlooking the River Nanny, and commanding the important river crossing. The new 'castellum' at Tuam was obviously designed to give protection to the growing monastic centre there as well as controlling traffic on the strategic routeway into Connacht.

The major architectural and artistic legacy of this period is undoubtedly the Romanesque cathedral and the high crosses. Of the cathedral, only the chancel with its chancel arch now survives, incorporated into the Protestant cathedral of St Mary. Despite its sandwiched position, its magnificent chancel arch, stone-vaulted ceiling and three-lighted east window give a good impression of the scale and appearance of a twelfth-century Irish cathedral. Both the arch and windows are covered in fine Romanesque carvings, dominated by foliage, chevron patterns and animal designs. Roger Stalley has dated the construction of this church to the years 1184-90. Though this is based partly on stylistic grounds, it also relies on a laconic entry in the *Annals of Loch Cé* for the year 1184. This records that 'the great church of Tuaim-da-ghualann fell in one day, both roof and stone'. The surviving remains are thus part of the rebuilt cathedral. Of the earlier cathedral, no structural remains are now visible. However, the thirteenth-century church of Temple Jarlath (already mentioned), which lies close by to the north-east, does contain a number of re-used stones with human heads carved in high relief. These come from a Romanesque arch, and may be the last vestiges of the earlier cathedral, possibly dating to 1172.

Of the four high crosses, that which stood until recently in the Market Square of Tuam is the best known. However, it has long been recognised that the head of this cross does not match the shaft. In fact, the three portions from which it is made up had originally been assembled from various points in the town for display at the Great Industrial Exhibition, held in Dublin in 1853. Upon their return to Tuam, they became the focus of a niggling sectarian struggle between the Church of Ireland and Catholic authorities over their possession and location. Finally, in 1874 they were formally erected at the Market Square, a symbolically neutral territory almost equidistant from the two cathedrals.

Having survived the attentions of nineteenth-century clerics, and frustrated the dreams of antiquarians to assemble one gigantic cross, all the cross fragments are now assembled in St Mary's cathedral. Having clocked up more moves than a team of moving statues, they can now be fully appreciated for the first time. From the inscriptions carved on the base and sides of the two surviving shafts, it appears that two of the crosses were constructed between 1128 and 1156. The third and fourth crosses, represented only by the cross heads, are probably of mid-twelfth and early thirteenth-century vintage.

As a group, the decoration on these crosses and the cathedral reveals the vibrant character of Irish stone carving throughout the twelfth century. Moreover, the carvings illustrate the originality of the western sculptors, who drew their inspiration from a number of sources, adapting motifs from the Irish and Viking traditions as well as from the English Romanesque. In the words of Roger Stalley, 'the importance of Tuam [is] as a foyer of [twelfth-century] Irish art and the richness of its artistic possessions'.

By the dawn of the thirteenth century, therefore, Tuam had become one of the foremost ecclesiastical centres in Ireland. What exactly the settlement looked like at this time is unclear, but we can paint a rough picture of its layout and extent. It appears to have been focused around the two ecclesiastical enclosures surrounding Temple Jarlath and Templenascreen. These may also have contained the residence of the archbishop and the guesthouse. Two high crosses probably stood on or just outside their circumference, one possibly marking the site of a market place. These enclosures were situated on the low ridge immediately to the south of the ford on the River Nanny. Between them, and overlooking the ford itself, was a major military fortification. A watermill probably stood on the river bank nearby. A short distance to the south-east of Temple Jarlath was the priory of St John, while to the south-west stood the Romanesque cathedral. Just beyond it, a newly founded house of the Premonstratensian order, known as the abbey of the Holy Trinity, was being built. Standing amidst these structures was at least one other high cross, as well as the humble houses of the lay tenants, artisans and servants, each with their adjoining yards and paddocks. Finally, at a distance of 800 metres or so to the south-east of this cluster was a third ecclesiastical enclosure at Toberjarlath.

When exactly Tuam made the transition from monastic settlement to monastic town is unclear, but the process was certainly well advanced by this time and would seem to have been complete by the mid-thirteenth century. The abbey of the Holy Trinity, probably founded in 1203-4, is described *c.*1211 as being situated 'in the suburbs of the metropolis of Tuam'. Moreover, in 1244, the *Annals* record that 'Tuam and all its churches were burnt and the houses of the whole town along with them'. Finally, in 1252, we read that Archbishop Flann McFlynn had received a licence to hold an annual fair at Tuam. Such historical references can be read as signposts indicating the presence of urban life.

Unfortunately, monastic towns like Tuam tend to lack the conventional criteria used to identify a medieval town, such as an urban charter, a planned street pattern, and formal defences. However, the absence of these elements can be misleading, for monastic towns were essentially major ceremonial rather than commercial or military centres. Thus, the criteria for identifying a monastic town are most likely to be the presence of a cathedral, the cult of a saint, public monuments like high crosses, as well as such ancillaries as a market and a seat of political power. The nearest Irish parallel in a modern context is perhaps Knock, in County Mayo, where the life and economy of the town centre around the shrine and the pilgrims it attracts.

Once established as a premier church centre, Tuam survived the upheavals of the Anglo-Norman invasion and the consequent decline of its chief patrons, the O'Connors. Though raided as early as 1177 by the Anglo-Normans, its status as the church's administrative capital of Connacht was never seriously questioned by the colonists. However, after its spectacular growth in the twelfth century, the succeeding 300 years mark a period of relative stagnation. In the early thirteenth century, Temple Jarlath had been rebuilt as a commodious parish church and a tower was added at its west end in the fifteenth century. It and Templenascreen now became the parish churches of two separate but adjoining parishes. Apart from this, however, the only other major building project was the construction of the large rectangular building at the west end of St Mary's cathedral between 1289 and 1312. Known as the Synod Hall, it appears to have been part of a bold but unfinished scheme of Archbishop William de Bermingham to rebuild the whole cathedral.

If the twelfth century witnessed the growth of Tuam as a monastic town, the seventeenth probably marked its emergence as a modern one. In 1613, James I issued charters to more than forty towns in Ireland including Tuam. While this was done for political and monetary motives, it gave the town an urban constitution for the first time. It also appears to have resulted in the extensive remodelling of its layout. The principal feature in the new scheme was the triangular Market Square from which five streets radiated. These included two completely new streets, High Street and Shop Street. Running westwards, High Street cut through the old monastic enclosure around Temple Jarlath. To the north ran Shop Street sloping downhill to a new bridge across the River Nanny, and eclipsing the old crossing point further downstream. With the construction of the new palace and demesne by the Protestant archbishop, Dr Edward Synge, in the earlier part of the eighteenth century, Bishop Street was also widened. Finally, to the south ran the Dublin Road and Vicar Street, the latter skirting the original market place at the Shambles. When exactly the subsidiary street known as The Mall was laid out is unclear. However, the other side street in this area, Circular Road, was not created until the mid-eighteenth century.

By the late eighteenth century, the town had developed into an important trading centre in the county, second only to Galway. A market house had been completed by 1718, and the chief industrial concerns included a brewery, three tanneries, at least two watermills and a pair of windmills. These and other trades served a growing agricultural population in the surrounding countryside, and by 1837 the town itself numbered 6,883 souls.

With the relaxation of the penal laws, a Catholic seminary, St Jarlath's College, was established in 1814, and just over a decade later, the first stones of the new Catholic cathedral were laid on the eve of Catholic emancipation. Tuam's rising fortunes in this period are mirrored in the proposals, albeit unrealised, to establish one of the new Queen's Colleges there. It eventually materialised in Galway. However, with its ecclesiastical background, Tuam was to become a major centre for first and second level education. Most of its extraordinary number of modern schools, nine in all, can trace their origins back to this period. After the great famine, Tuam, like many provincial towns, witnessed the slow haemorrhaging of its population to emigration. However, with the laying of the foundation stone of the present town hall in 1857, and the coming of the railway in 1860, the town maintained its status as a routeway and market centre well into the twentieth century.

Today, Tuam is a compact market town in the plains of north Galway. Its modern industrial base includes microchips, electrical engineering and textiles. However, the recent loss of the sugar factory, its main employer since the 1930s, has been a major body blow. Its population has been contracting steadily since, down by no less than 16 per cent between 1986 and 1991 to its present total of 3,448. Tuam, however, is a stoical place, where the citizens or 'Shams' still delight in the town's remarkable *floruit* in the twelfth century, while enduring the problems of the twentieth.

Select bibliography
H. Dutton: *A Statistical and Agricultural Survey of the County of Galway*, Dublin, 1824
R. J. Kelly: 'The old borough of Tuam: its laws, privileges, and constitution', *Journal of the Galway Archaeological and Historical Society*, iv (1906), pp. 233-9
J. A. Claffey: 'The history of the high cross of Tuam', seven parts, *Tuam Herald*, March-April 1966
D. S. Ó Murchú: *Tuaim*, Tuam, 1970
R. Stalley: 'The Romanesque sculpture of Tuam', in A. Barg and A. Martindle (eds), *The Vanishing Past*, British Archaeological Reports, International Series 3, Oxford, 1981, pp. 179-95 and plates 1-19
L. Swan: 'Monastic proto-towns in early medieval Ireland: the evidence of aerial photography, plan analysis and survey', in H. B. Clarke and A. Simms (eds), *The Comparative History of Urban Origins in Non-Roman Europe*, BAR International Series 255 i, 1985, pp. 77-102

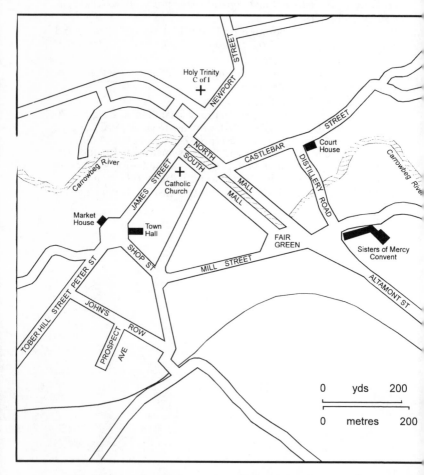

Westport, based on Ordnance Survey Road Atlas of Ireland, 1985

WESTPORT

Desmond McCabe

LIKE many of the smaller Irish towns, Westport, County Mayo, is quite young. It made the transition from a cosy, untidy village to an ordered town of great charm just over 200 years ago. The fabric of the town has changed little since the 1800s, but the irony is that evidence of continuous occupation of homes and premises can call up a deeper sense of the lapse of time than can signs of more thorough change or upheaval. The sea no longer plays an important part in the life of the town. But, to the 1950s, townspeople kept up a wide range of overseas contacts, as ships from abroad regularly called to the port. The modern tourist trade has its roots as far back as the 1800s. The existence of the town and these aspects of its social and commercial life derive in some measure from the designs and activity of several generations of the Browne family who have been resident in Cathair na Mart from the 1650s. However, although the town is one of the most elegant examples of the planned landlord town in the country, the contribution of local masons and contractors to the architecture of its streets was very considerable. In this short essay I will focus particularly on the origins and development of the town from the 1760s to the 1820s.

Travellers have commented on the prettiness of the town and its situation since the 1780s. Its shelving streetscape, with delicately stepped houses and footpaths, is very attractive, though it must be said that Quay Street, Tobberhill and High Street make good climbs. The tree-lined Mall has been universally admired. In the early part of the last century, travellers by carriage would usually have come down the old Castlebar road and crossed the river at the bottom of Bridge Street. If the visitor were in town on business he would probably have ridden down the Mall and up James Street to the Octagon where farmers and weavers brought their goods for sale. Purchases on any scale were carted down the long road to the quay, along the 15-foot-high

Westport in c. 1818 by James Arthur O'Connor, British Museum, London

demesne wall of Westport House, for storage in one of the warehouses there. From the later 1860s railway travellers passed down Altamont Street, under the railway bridge (on the Newport line), past the walls of the convent of the Sisters of Mercy to the right, and the expanse of the old fair green to the left. Straight ahead, the road dipped down to the North Mall, and the Railway Hotel, a reputable inn since the 1790s.

The period of most rapid and extensive construction in Westport was between 1775 and 1815. This period can be divided into two phases. The initial phase was from 1775 to 1800, when the Octagon or market place formed the social and architectural pivot of the town. The second phase was defined essentially by the creation of a mall in the lower part of the town between 1800 and about 1815. Properly speaking, the whole town now consisted of the complex which is made up of the main town itself, the streets and harbour at

Westport Quay, and the demesne and mansion of Westport House, all of which were inter-related.

Though there were habitations about the area of Cathair na Mart as far back as 3,000 B.C., the place was not a centre of any importance in the middle ages. It lay on an ancient route of pilgrimage to the sacred mountain of Croagh Patrick. The chieftains of the O'Malleys dominated the area until the later middle ages and supported a castle in Cathair na Mart (or 'the stone fort of the beeves') until it was burnt down by crown forces in 1583. In the 1640s the territory came into the possession of John Browne, an able and adventurous soldier and lawyer. Browne took up residence there, near the old village, in the 1650s, but had changed the name of his address from 'Cahernamart' to the more respectable or less Gaelic-sounding 'Westport', by the 1680s. Very little is known of the place at this period. Browne maintained an ironworks near his residence where tools and weapons were made and no doubt the village would have contained craftsmen, farm servants and fishermen.

Roads were primitive in the seventeenth century and communication by sea was often more efficient. There was little trade in the county and rents were generally paid in kind on the Browne estate. The family remained Catholic until the conversion of John Browne, son of Peter Browne, who died in 1724. A small 'masshouse' was therefore tolerated in the village in 1715. The accession of John Browne to the estate after his father's death, marked the beginning of a period of stability in family fortunes and the start of a century-long development of the area. The half-ruined house at Westport was restored and fitted with an impressive Georgian east front by the architect Richard Cassels in 1730. A small Protestant church, now in ruins, was built on the demesne. Some years later Bishop Pococke visited John Browne in 1752. At this point the original village was undisturbed but grandiose plans were in the air for its removal and the construction of a new town and demesne park. It is likely that crucial decisions were made in the late 1760s. Like many landlords, Browne wished to make a steady profit out of his estate, and the conventional wisdom of the time was for the landlord to get an export trade of some sort going among his tenantry in order to bring cash into the estate. Like Charles Bingham of Castlebar and others he encouraged the growth of flax, the spinning of yarn and the weaving of linen on his estate.

A new market place was required for a healthy textile trade. The old village was dismantled and houses were laid out a mile or so away on the present site of Westport. Some of the earliest slate-roofed, two-storey houses, with small windows, remain on High Street, Peter Street and Bridge Street. In the early 1770s a vast quantity of slates was imported to Westport as construction commenced. The erection of slated town houses reflected well in contemporary eyes on the initiative and the social standing of the landlord responsible. These early residences were built by local craftsmen for weavers encouraged to live there by the offer of long-term leases at low rents. It is likely, all the same, that the shape taken by the streets was in accordance with the vision of John Browne, now the first earl of Altamont. By the early 1780s the Octagon was the focal point of the town. This fact is visible from the road map of George Taylor and Andrew Skinner in 1778. John Wesley preached in Westport about this time, making a detour from a trip to Newport. The town was now socially on the map. One of the most significant buildings dating from this period is the market house with its four-arched, cut-stone exterior. Though James Wyatt designed the west front of Westport House about this time it is doubtful if he or any other well-known architect was involved in the disposition of the streets or the erection of this or other buildings.

As weavers and others were accommodated in the rising town the earl of Altamont saw to the regulation and promotion of trade. Again, like other landlords in such remote areas, Altamont was obliged to act as sole merchant buyer and exporter in the infant years of the textile trade. Tenants were given discounts off their rent if they produced yarn and linen for the stores of the earl. But, by the mid-1770s, Altamont had persuaded outside merchants to settle in the town and take a chance with the trade. Robert Patten from

Belfast appears to have been the first merchant to come. Then came Charles Higgins and Charles MacDonnell and the Presbyterian merchants, Richard Livingstone and William Pinkerton.

One of the urgent priorities now, and something which Altamont must have discussed with these new merchants, was to make the small quay at the river mouth suitable for large-scale traffic. At this period the port of Newport-Pratt, some miles away, was of more real consequence than Westport, having superior natural facilities. However, it declined in the face of the determination and capital investment of the earl of Altamont. The port was deepened and a solid quay wall built. The gloomy, forbidding warehouses of MacDonnell and others were put up in the early 1780s. Still to be seen on one warehouse is a stone inscribed with the date 1783 and the initials of Charles MacDonnell. Linen cloth and yarn bought up in the new market were stored here for shipping out to Glasgow and the north of Ireland. The value of textile sales had risen to £10,000 in Westport by 1776 from a base of almost nothing in 1772. Local farmers grew and processed flax, and then spun yarn in order to sell it to weavers in the market house on the Octagon. Weavers turned the yarn into webs of coarse linen cloth for display and sale to the agents of local and northern merchants. The webs were then carted to the warehouses at the quay and piled up for export. This round of labour continued until the trade fell into decay in the 1820s. The amount of employment given by the trade was striking and certainly the prosperity of the town and neighbourhood was borne in on travellers in the 1780s and 1790s. Margins earned locally on the sale of both yarn and linen were not however very high and prosperity was in large measure due to rents not having caught up with the modest local gains in income. Merchants of the time made considerable profits, through the operation of a cartel on the local market, and through diversification into the profitable herring fishery of the 1780s. Masses of salt herring would also have taken up space in the warehouses in these years. The long-term prospects for domestic textiles were quite uncertain and Patten and Livingstone in particular were happy to turn to the export of oats and oatmeal in the late 1790s.

By the early 1780s then, the town was established in its first phase. The Reverend Daniel and Mrs Beaufort visited here in 1787 and liked the aspect of the town and were startled by the speed of its growth. Mastery of county politics on the part of the Browne family ensured that the town continued to be favoured. Allegations were widespread at the time that the first marquess of Sligo (raised from earl of Altamont in 1801) lavished an undue share of county funds into the continued development of port and town. There was probably a grain of truth in such charges – the Browne family acted on the Mayo grand jury much as all major county families in Ireland did at this time. The nature of trade in the town changed after the declaration of war against France by England in 1793. The market for provisions and cheap cloth increased enormously in order to satisfy the needs of troops campaigning against the armies of the French Revolution and then the armies of Napoleon. Merchants in Westport exploited capital accumulated in the linen trade to invest in the export of corn from Mayo. During the 1790s corn exports were minimal. Small farmers carried sacks of corn to vessels at the quay and were given discounts off their rent as in the early days of the linen trade. Exports rose rapidly in the 1800s and merchants experienced a boom in business during the Peninsular war of 1808 to 1813. Over 12,000 tons of oats left Westport each year between September and December. Twenty ships were registered to town merchants at the port.

One merchant, Robert Patten, was said to have made vast sums by the export of calicoes, corn and salted pork to Spain. At first, Patten sent the calicoes and oats separately to the Spanish ports, but he found that the Spanish authorities taxed the import of calicoes. The story goes that he evaded Spanish customs and increased his profits by packing the oats in calico sacks for the rest of the war. Army tailors had no difficulty turning the sacks into shirts. A story was also told of how Richard Livingstone and the first marquess of Sligo jogged down the quay on their horses in the summer of

1809 talking of the profits on the corn trade with wonder and satisfaction. At this period the quay was greatly extended and a number of massive warehouses six or seven storeys high were erected to cater for the several trades. The channel by the quay was deepened to admit ships of 200 tons in burden to a mooring. The neat customs house with its half-moon windows was built in the early 1800s to act as an office for the various customs officials of the port. By 1813 the business of the port was at its height in terms of profits. A painting of the harbour in 1818 by James Arthur O'Connor, commissioned by the first marquess of Sligo, gives us an impression of leisurely activity on a normal day outside the rushed season of winter export. Three single-masted coasting vessels stand in the harbour. One is unfurling its sails to leave port. Labourers trundle barrels, or hogsheads, landed from two of the ships, and carry planks to store in one of the warehouses, under the supervision of a frock-coated man with his hands on his hips. One large warehouse, at the corner of Quay Road, has not yet been roofed. A yacht, possibly belonging to the first marquess, lies at rest on the water. The buildings of the quay are much as they are today. Large vessels could not approach the quay wall, but would anchor out towards Islandmore or Inislyre, in deep water, and lighters would take goods to or from them. Men from the small islands outside the harbour acted as pilots for these vessels.

As the business of the quay expanded, the second phase of town development was undertaken. Primarily, this entailed the creation of the present Mall. It seems that Altamont had envisaged the creation of a mall during the late 1780s, but it was not until the early 1800s that the plan could be realised. The profits of trade were ploughed into the project. It was rumoured in 1808 that the first marquess had spent over £25,000 on the town and demesne in that decade. By the early 1800s, two or three oat mills, a flour mill, a brewery and a threshing mill had been raised in the town and quay. The grassy road from Castlebar to Westport was turned into a gravelled mail coach road. In 1787 the Reverend Charles Lynagh received a lease on a plot for a proposed new Catholic chapel. Funds were not available to make a start on the structure until 1813. The line of buildings along the Mall was more or less in place by the 1800s however. Over the next few years the River Carrowbeg was made to flow shallowly between dressed stone walls and over flagstones, to produce a boulevard effect of great originality in the Irish urban context. Frederick Trench was captivated by the town Mall in late 1814, and found the town incomparably neat and effective in its arrangement of houses. At one end of the Mall stood a new entrance to the enlarged and beautified demesne. Townspeople were free to stroll in the demesne at all times.

By the early 1820s the population of the town and quay had attained about 4,300 and some 500 houses lined the streets. The small urban landscape here was really quite new. To serve the consumption needs of the merchants, craftsmen, artisans and others in the new town, numbers of small shops had begun to appear. These premises started by importing goods for the immediate vicinity, but were eventually to act as centres of distribution much further afield. However, the depression of trade which followed the end of the Napoleonic wars in 1815 meant that to all intents and purposes the impetus for town construction petered out. There was little addition to the fabric of the town before the great famine. In fact, in many respects, the town remained in the form it reached about 1820, until further developments commenced in the 1930s. Between 1813 and 1821 the old Catholic chapel was completed at a cost of £6,000. The fanciful, castellated facade, which has long since disappeared, faced across the Mall to Robinson's Hotel (later the Railway Hotel). At the invitation of George Clendinning, agent to the first marquess of Sligo, the Bank of Ireland established one of the first of its branches outside the capital in Westport in 1825.

By the 1830s the linen trade of the town had collapsed. Power spinning in the north of Ireland had put spinners of yarn out of work in the west by 1825. The market for the coarse linen of the area was quickly undermined. Rent was now paid by the sale of oats and livestock. There was less

140

surplus income to spend in the town and poverty grew among craftsmen and labourers. The export of corn reached record levels in Westport in the years before the famine, and gave some employment to labouring families in the town, but this trade did not reflect a healthy regional economy. The building of a workhouse in 1841-2, and a new courthouse in 1842, to cope with increased sessions business, relate in different ways to the distress of the times. The foundation stone of the workhouse, which contained a gold sovereign and a Father Mathew temperance medal, was laid on the left hand side of the road to the quay in August 1841. The poor law union struggled from year to year during the famine of 1845 to 1850. The town was a venue for perishing individuals and families seeking relief. Many inhabitants of the town and its hinterland died of starvation or of fever, or emigrated. Evictions by the second marquess of Sligo controversially accompanied the disaster. The town was at a low ebb in the early 1850s.

It was more than a decade after the famine before the town began to recover. Agricultural prosperity in the 1860s meant that shopkeepers and craftsmen in Westport could survive and look to the future. Gas lighting was introduced in the late 1850s. When the Earl and Countess Spencer came to Westport by train, in 1869, they were greeted by bonfires, a profusion of banners, and, on the gable of one house, 'the figure of a transparent harp, supplied with gas'. Town commissioners maintained macadamised roads and flagged footpaths. The major innovation of the period was the development of a railway service, by the Midland Great Western Railway, from Castlebar to Westport. The line was proposed in the early 1860s and £15,000 invested towards its completion by the second marquess of Sligo. Westport station opened in February 1866. By the 1870s substantial shopkeepers in Westport distributed goods of a wide variety wholesale to many parts of the county and province. Imports included timber from North America and the Baltic, Indian corn from the Black Sea and the United States, coal, iron, tea, sugar, coffee, and manufactured articles of all sorts from Glasgow and Liverpool. By this period, tinned and packaged groceries

141

and mass-produced clothes had begun to be retailed. Perhaps the most substantial user of the quay, and the largest trader in town, was the merchant and importing concern of William Livingstone, which had consolidated its business in Westport from the 1790s. This family operated a distillery on Distillery Road in the town from 1826 to the 1890s, closing only for a brief period during the temperance movement of 1840 to 1842. Quay business gave a cosmopolitan character to the town for many years. Port trade lost vitality at the turn of the century and was killed off by the economic war of 1932 to 1938, and by world-wide changes in goods transport before the Second World War. The last foreign sailing vessel to unload at the quay was the 400-ton schooner *Frida* in April 1934.

A growing feature of the town from the 1860s was the development of tourism. In the early 1800s, the first marquess of Sligo had aspired to make the town a resort for sea-bathers and had installed warm water baths at the quay. As late as 1883 these facilities were still on offer at the rate of one guinea per person for a season ticket. Tourists also came each summer to stay in bathing lodges on the shores of Clew Bay. The present Railway Hotel was established by the first marquess deliberately to draw visitors. For a time in the 1870s entrepreneurs in the town ran a steamship excursion service around Clew Bay and to the cliffs of Achill. A clear line of continuity runs therefore from the speculative designs of the first marquess of Sligo in the 1800s to the present extensive development of tourism in and about Westport.

The trade which formed the basis of the town during its development and construction has altered irrevocably. The Livingstone family, who were the last of the original merchant families of the town, moved from the area in the early years of this century. New industries such as mariculture and the making of pharmaceuticals have emerged. Some of the old warehouses have been refurbished to serve as hostels and hotels. The lines of town development are still clear. Numbers of the families who lived in the town in the 1850s and 1860s are represented in the town or area today. In the language of the old Westport cattle-dealers, we may wish centuries more change and continuity to new and old 'covey' or 'residenter' families of the town.

Select bibliography

Marquess of Sligo: *Westport House and the Brownes*, Ashbourne, Derbyshire, 1981

R. Gillespie and G. Moran (eds): *'A Various Country': Essays in Mayo History, 1500-1900*, Westport, 1987

P. Ó Flanagain: 'An outline history of the town of Westport, part I: the origins and early development of the town of Westport, 1750-1780', *Cathair na Mart: Journal of the Westport Historical Society*, i (1) (1981), pp. 5-12

P. Ó Flanagain:'An outline history of the town of Westport, part II: Westport – a new town 1780-1825', *Cathair na Mart: Journal of the Westport Historical Society*, ii (1) (1982), pp. 35-52

John Mulloy: 'Some aspects of trade in Clew Bay, part I', *Cathair na Mart: Journal of the Westport Historical Society*, xi (1991), pp. 57-64

John Mulloy: 'Some aspects of trade in Clew Bay, part II', *Cathair na Mart: Journal of the Westport Historical Society*, xii (1992), pp. 55-60

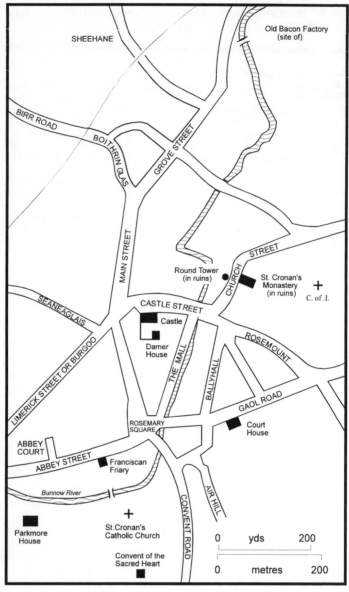

Roscrea, based on Ordnance Survey of Ireland, six inches to one mile,
1954

144

ROSCREA

George Cunningham

WHAT have the likes of Saints Molua and Carthage, Gerald Barry of Wales, Henry of London, Aodh and Eoin Rua O'Neill, Thomas Moore, Father Mathew, Pope Paul VI, Arlo Guthrie, Tom Paxton and President Mary Robinson got in common? Well for one thing they all visited Roscrea, if only briefly. But countless others have hurried through this north Tipperary town shaking their heads in exasperation at being held up by its narrow winding streets.

Since Early Christian times Roscrea has been situated at a crossroads of one of the five great roads of ancient Ireland, the Slí Dhála, the road of the Assemblies – part of today's N7, the primary route to Limerick and the mid-west. The north-south route from the town grew as a roadway of equal if not greater importance: a midland corridor joining the monastic midlands and such famous monasteries as Durrow, Rahan, Lynally, Drumcullen, Kinnitty and Seir Kieran with Cashel and Derrynaflan to the south. Indeed all communications in and out of the south-west midlands were channelled through this Roscrea gap, on the edge of extensive bogland and between the Slieve Bloom and the Devilsbit Mountains in the territory known as O'Carroll's country, Éile or Ely O'Carroll.

St Cronan, a native of the area, founded his first monastery one mile east of the present town, in what was then a remote secluded woody spot as its name Sean Ross implies. Because travellers had great difficulty in locating this monastery and its guesthouse, Cronan was persuaded to move alongside the highway. So, on the rising ground between present-day Church Street and Rosemount a new monastery was founded in the late sixth century. It prospered and grew, eventually evolving as our modern town. But of the fledgling settlement or proto-town we know very little. The twentieth-century street plan tells us little about its extent

Roscrea, the Market Square at the beginning of the twentieth century
(photograph property of George Cunningham)

and nothing remains *in situ* of the original monastery.

The various annals have many entries for Cronan's Roscrea emphasising its importance. These, in the main, record the deaths of the abbots but raids by Norsemen are related on three occasions. One of these in 845 became the celebrated battle of Roscrea at which the local monks, traders and townspeople inflicted a heavy defeat on the 'foreigners of Limerick' who had tried to plunder Aonach Éile, the great fair of Ely O'Carroll. Although nothing is now visible of the original monastery, artefacts housed elsewhere point to various high-quality activities in stone, metalwork and manuscript. Noteworthy are the *Gospel Book of Dimma* and the Roscrea Brooch both dated to around 800.

In 1111 at the synod of Rathbreasail the O'Carrolls, patrons of St Cronan's, were not powerful enough for the O'Brien dynasty of Dál gCáis and so Roscrea lost its claim to become an independent diocese; St Cronan's and its extensive termon lands became part of the diocese of Killaloe. Roscrea ignored the synodal decision and went about asserting its independence in a formidable manner: the notable monastic ruins of church, cross and tower, valuable manuscripts and the shrine of the *Book of Dimma* all date from this time, pointing to almost feverish activity to emphasise the claim for diocesan status. All that remains now of the cathedral church of this diocese of Éile or Ros Cré is the exquisite Hiberno-Romanesque west gable. Modelled on Cormac's Cashel its sandstone decorative features are now weathering badly. The nearby three-metre-tall high cross is unusual both in concept and design. Today's N7 cuts the monastery in two, isolating the round tower on the other side of the road. Its one-masted sailing ship carved in bold relief inside the east window is noteworthy. It is indeed ironic that the most landlocked town in Ireland should have one of the earliest pictorial representations of a sailing ship. What navigational problems the Roscrea monks had in the twelfth century remain sadly unimaginable!

Manuscript survivals from that pulsating century include the *Annals of Roscrea*, the *Rule of Echtgus Ua Cuanáin* and the *Life of St Cronan*. As Roscrea was represented as a diocese at the synod of Kells in 1152 these efforts to achieve independence were partly successful, but only for the lifetime of the then bishop; following his death Ros Cré once again was amalgamated with Killaloe, becoming a deanery of Éile in that diocese.

With the arrival of the Augustinian canons and then the Anglo-Normans, the monastery became parochial with the cathedral church of St Cronan functioning as the parish church. It continued to do so until 1812 when a new place of worship for the Church of Ireland community was built. Because of its antiquity and great beauty the west gable was preserved and allowed to stand, acting as a sort of lychgate to the new building.

Prior to 1200 no evidence of settlement survives in the town other than at the monastic site at Church Street. In the early thirteenth century the focus swung to the high ground a little to the west of the monastery. By then Roscrea's crossroads situation and its strategic position inevitably led to its fortification. Due to many disturbances in the Irish midlands the Anglo-Norman army and council assembled at Roscrea in 1213 and decided to construct a royal castle there. The site chosen at Roscrea was an excellent one for their earthen motte and bailey: on the high ground of a moraine above a river controlling a major route – the area of ground now between the Mall, Castle Street and the top half of Rosemary Street. Unfortunately for them it was part of the ancient termon lands of St Cronan's lately acquired by the bishop of Killaloe. On hearing of the proposal to build he came hotfoot to Roscrea and threatened excommunication on all, including the justiciar, Archbishop Henry of London, if they didn't desist. They begged him for the common good to allow the fortification to remain, promising compensation. As it took almost seventy years for this to be paid the earthen castle – probably located to the rear of the present post office – survived until the 1280s when the adjoining stone castle was erected.

This royal castle was state-of-the-art for its time: a keepless stronghold with a moated defended gate tower, two D-shaped corner turrets and linking curtain walls. Its soft interior buildings have not survived but it is probable that the courtyard was cluttered with all the paraphernalia necessary for medieval warfare. In 1280 compensation was paid to the bishop of Killaloe not only for the castle site but for the termon lands of St Cronan which then became the manor of Roscrea with burgesses paying £6 13s 4d per annum for some 12 $1/2$ carucates of land – about 1,500 acres.

Like so many other non-chartered settlements Roscrea

presents us with a virtual documentary black hole for the medieval period making it extremely difficult to estimate its importance or its size. Certainly the new manor flourished in the thirteenth century. By then Monaincha, two miles east of the town, had become internationally famous as a place of pilgrimage. And pilgrims needed provisions. The presence of an Ostman community in the town hints at commercial enterprises. In 1254 the *villata* of Roscrea had to pay ten marks for injustice in that a certain man was falsely hanged and for false measure. The stone castle must have generated much wealth: in 1278 the wages of carpenters, masons, quarrymen and the cost of iron and lead used amounted to over £363. In 1281, the state papers tell us, the king's army came to Roscrea for nine days 'to procure provisions and to guard the country'. A few years later the army of Roscrea – a sort of compulsory national levy – was proclaimed. The king's prison for the emerging county of Tipperary was in Roscrea castle; recent excavations have located part of the gaol under the ground floor of the gate tower. In 1295 some 39 persons were delivered to Clonmel for a hearing. Justice was of a summary nature: of the 24 found guilty 18 were hanged. But at least the castle and manor were prospering.

So what of the layout of the town in the early fourteenth century? The main manorial mill was probably at Church Street near the round tower. From there, the river unchannelled ran across what is now Lower Castle Street and lapped the walls of the castle from the drawbridge down the street which became the Mall. On the higher ground Rosemary Street and Square were part of the castle orchards and gardens. Even down to the nineteenth century these areas were known as Kingsland. Modern townlands such as Demesne, Townparks, Parkmore, Glebe hint at medieval settlement behind their nineteenth-century garb. Main Street, Limerick Street, Grove Street and Bóithrín Glas developed from the burgage plots of the burgesses. 'Burgoo', the alternative name for Limerick Street, hints at a corruption of 'burgage' or 'borough'. East of the river became known as Ballyhall, *Baile Thall*, 'the town over there', and may well have been the Irishtown of the manor.

Granted to the Ormond Butlers in 1315, the formidable fortress of the castle assured their survival over the following centuries. Indeed, until the advent of strong cannon it remained impregnable. But the unwalled town was at the mercy of the strong Gaelic resurgence of the O'Carrolls of the later fourteenth and fifteenth centuries and any expansion or even consolidation of settlement seems to have proved difficult. However, the town survived: its reeve and community are mentioned in 1399 and again in 1432. The subsequent arrival of a mendicant order extending the built-up area to present-day Abbey Street, certainly points to a sizeable population.

The Franciscans came to Roscrea during the latter half of the fifteenth century. A tombstone within the church told: 'Pray for the soul of Maolruny O'Carroll, lord of Ely and prince of Ireland, at that time 1523; it was he who caused me to be built'. An O'Carroll foundation within a stone's throw of a major Butler castle and in the heart of a Butler manor remains puzzling. We know that the Franciscans had arrived in Roscrea before 1477. In that year Prior Ruaidhrí of nearby Lorrha recorded that the friars minor with some of the O'Carrolls gathered in Roscrea and not only looted the church of Cronan but also the fine church and new residence of their patron St Francis, 'and from all these places they carried away much booty: fine clothing, sides of beef, sides of ham, great cuts of mutton both boiled in water and roasted, venison roasted in a kind of butter and a variety of beverages: wine and whiskey, mead and beer beyond measure ... and in the name of St Francis they ate and drank ...' – two or three words, doubtlessly describing worse excesses, are completely rubbed out at this point. It must have been an interesting evening in the town!

I suspect that Maolruny and his wife Bibiana made a subsequent endowment around 1490 in reparation for these deeds; certainly the belfry is a later insertion and dates from that time. The friary was short-lived: we have no record of the dissolution but an inquisition of 1568 found that the precincts covered two acres. It remained a ruin until early in the nineteenth century when a pre-emancipation Roman

Catholic chapel was erected within the site. The building now known as the Legion Hall or the Library is all that remains of this church. The belfry acts as a modern gateway to the imposing Roman Catholic parish church which dates from 1844 although it was not roofed until 1855.

In the seventeenth century the commercial life of the town began to expand. In 1633 Charles I granted the fairs and tolls to the earl of Ormond 'for the public good of our subjects living in or near the town or manor of Roscrea ... so that the rude and wild people of the district may be brought to a human and civilised kind of life, and more easily obtain provision of all things necessary'! The Civil Survey gives this potted picture of the town in 1641: 'At the town of Roscrea is a large castle and a bawn in repair, many thatched cottages and cabins, a ruined large abbey, a corn mill upon a brook, a market weekly on Thursday, a fair twice a year on Midsummer and Michaelmas Day ... customary manorial courts ... and all privileges belonging to a manor'.

Petty's 1659 tax poll of adults counted 57 soldiers and their wives in the castle and 93 Irish and 11 English in the town; and shortly afterwards another record lists 106 householders paying the two shillings tax per hearth per annum. A market house was erected soon afterwards in Market Square. A Birr lease of 1671 directed that a market house was to be built in Birr 'as good as is built in Roscrea'.

By the beginning of the eighteenth century the Butlers had lost their demesnes and manors: Roscrea town and castle were mortgaged to various interests before becoming the property of the Damers. Later through marriage this family became the Dawson-Damers, the earls of Portarlington. These wealthy Damers, the richest people in Ireland at that time, opened up the town, channelled the river away from the castle's walls to create the Mall and sold the castle's orchards for the commercial development that created Rosemary Street and Square. These new public areas of the town were reputedly named after two Damer ladies, prompting a local wag later to write:

Some say the town is not kept clean
And smells to a degree

151

But surely no one can object
To the smells of Rosemary.

Damer's town house, built in the middle of the castle court-yard around 1720, is not only of great architectural merit but is now synonymous with the modern heritage awakening in Roscrea. This pre-palladian three-storey nine-bay house has a superb hand-carved pine staircase and many other features of note. In turn the house became a barracks, sanatorium, school, offices, library and a derelict site. Today, following a lengthy campaign to save and restore the building, it serves as a focal point for heritage development.

The eighteenth and early nineteenth centuries were periods of great growth in Roscrea, helped by its situation on the main coach roads. Much commercial building took place along the principal streets. By the 1830s and 1840s this growth was reflected in the new public buildings of schools, dispensary, bridewell and petty sessions on greenfield sites at Gaol Road. In 1839 the dispensary expended only £65, ministering to 4,101 patients. I'm sure our present minister of health would love to know the secret of how that was done! An extensive workhouse was erected on the Templemore Road in 1842. It and an auxiliary building at the foot of the Limerick Road were to cater for 2,000 inmates at the end of the famine. The large fever hospital on the Monastery Road while accommodating over 400 patients also acted as the mass burial plot for the countless harrowing deaths of those times.

In the 1820s, before the protective duty was removed, the woollen industry employed 1,000, of whom 600 or 700 were women, in the town and neighbourhood. Up to the repeal of the corn laws the trade in corn remained extensive. The trades of tanning, brogue-making, nailing, chandlery, brewing and distilling prospered up to the introduction of machinery and the railways. Roscrea whiskey – distilled by Birches – was one of the well-known brands before local events and Father Mathew, the apostle of temperance, sealed its fate; in 1850 the distillery was up for auction. Today a drop of Roscrea will cost you quite some pennies: four bottles were auctioned recently for £700. Many nineteenth-century visitors to the town have left varying accounts. T. L. Cooke, the Birr historian, writing in 1834, was both pleased and saddened by the town's appearance:

> I own I was both disappointed and disgusted on entering the town through a long and dirty lane, skirted on both sides with wretched and unseemly cabins ... I proceeded to a wide street leading to the Market House ... rubbish everywhere ... On enquiry I found that the town had the misfortune to belong to absentee landlords ... at present Roscrea is inhabited by a most deserving and industrious race of people worthy of a benign and encouraging landlord.

Cooke's long and dirty lane was the present Birr Road. The plots and cabins there were the probable survivors from the thirteenth-century borough and were eventually swept away in the 1850s when the large cutting for the railway – both the Parsonstown and the Limerick line – was made. Arriving in 1862 on a branch line from Ballybrophy the railway was both a boon for and the death knell of many traditional crafts and small cottage industries.

The absentee landlords referred to by Cooke squandered the rents from Roscrea in the gambling halls of London and Europe. So it was no surprise when in 1856 the entire town was for sale through the encumbered estates court. This led to much commercial development but did little for the wretched living conditions of the ordinary inhabitants of the town. It was not until 1898 when power was transferred from the Roscrea board of guardians to the rural district council that the removal of lanes and the clearance of the cabins at Burgoo, Bóithrín Glas and Railway View were tackled. Railway View was also known as Bunker's Hill – presumably called after the American battle – but for what reason we don't know. Rows of terraced cottages with verandas and houses with gabled hoods now graced these streets. In the 1920s, to allow for a freer flow of traffic along the route through the town, the Victorian fountain in the market square was removed to Rosemary and the fine market house itself was demolished.

But it took until the 1930s and 1940s for public housing at the Crescent, St Cronan's Terrace, Limerick Street and

Limerick Road to finally do away with all of the dated cabins. Today only one half-door survives in the town. Assumption Park, a new council housing estate north of the town, was built in the 1950s, followed by Kennedy Park, Cois Carraige, Seaneaglais and Sheehane. Up to recent times private housing development shunned the town centre and concentrated on ribbon building along all the approach roads. A notable exception was the small number of private houses built for factory personnel at Abbey Court. Moneen Court, the first large private housing scheme, is nearing completion in a former sandpit site on the Convent Hill.

The first convent in Ireland of the Sacred Heart Order was founded in Roscrea, in 1842, on Air Hill, across the road from that now vanished sandpit, building on the work of the Brigidines who had been teaching in the town since 1823. Their 150 years of celebration in 1992, graced with the attendance of the president of Ireland, was a milestone in the history of the area.

With a monastic tradition stretching from Early Christian times to the reformation it was only fitting that Ireland's second post-emancipation Cistercian monastery should be sited in Roscrea. In 1878, to the west of the town on lands once owned by the monks of Monaincha, the Cistercians of Melleray founded Mount Street Joseph Abbey. The population in the 1830s reached 9,000; the famine hit hard, but the real scourge from 1850 to the 1950s was emigration. By the turn of the century the townspeople numbered just over 2,500, but an increase of 45 per cent between 1901 and 1961 is among the highest in the country. Today's population is creeping towards the 5,000 figure although the day-time figure is much higher. Post-primary schools alone – CBS, convent and vocational – have enrolments in excess of 1,000.

In 1907 the first farmers' industrial co-operative in Ireland, Roscrea Bacon Factory, opened for business – its sunburst ham and sausages filled many an empty tummy. Today, now much expanded under the Avonmore umbrella, it continues to thrive in new premises under Carrick Hill. Beef processing (the Roscrea Casserole brand was a household name in Britain in the 1940s and 1950s), Antigen Pharmaceuticals and Offray Ribbon are the other main industries.

In recent days, the commercial life of the town received a welcome boost with the opening in 1992 of a major shopping centre, built at a rear junction of the two principal streets. It is indeed ironic that through traffic, the reason for Roscrea's growth from prehistoric times, is the town's greatest problem today. The Slí Dhála was never meant to carry the traffic of modern times and so the by-pass on the N7 which is nearing completion will allow the town to breathe again. Roscrea is now one of Ireland's designated heritage towns. For the past twenty years it has been to the forefront of all heritage developments in Ireland. Pioneering archaeological, environmental and genealogical schemes have emanated from the heritage centre at the Castle Complex and major restoration and conservation work is in progress spearheaded by a community and state partnership between the office of public works and the local heritage society. St Cronan's monastery is once again being presented in a fitting manner, the Franciscans will shortly get a face-lift and the drawbridge to the restored castle is once again down, this time ready to welcome all visitors to this historic town of Roscrea.

Select bibliography
D. Gleeson: *Roscrea Town and Parish*, Dublin, 1947
G. Cunningham: *Roscrea People*, Roscrea, 22 issues, 1974 to date
G. Cunningham: *Roscrea and District*, Roscrea, 1976
G. Cunningham: *Historic Roscrea*, Roscrea, 1983
K. Moloughney: *Roscrea Me Darlin'*, Roscrea, 1987
K. Moloughney: *Roscrea My Heart's Home*, Roscrea, 1992

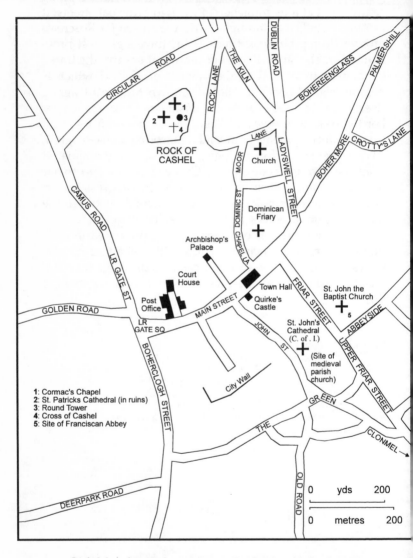

Cashel, based on Ordnance Survey Road Atlas of Ireland, 1985

CASHEL

Tadhg O'Keeffe

EVERYBODY who has travelled by road from Dublin to Cork knows that moment when the Rock of Cashel suddenly comes into view. It is a sensational sight: sticking out of a green, fertile lowland is this huge, bare, craggy rock with a busy cluster of medieval walls and towers rising out of the top of it, almost as if they are growing on it. This is Cashel of the Kings, the very heart of an ancient province of Munster, the centrepiece of Munster's historic landscape. For centuries, from the time of St Patrick up to about 200 years ago, the Rock was a stronghold, first of royal power, and then of ecclesiastical power. When most people think of Cashel today it is the Rock that comes to mind, but the town that has lived in the shadow of the Rock for the past eight centuries is no less interesting an historical document. Founded early in the thirteenth century by an archbishop rather than by a secular lord, it is a model example of an Anglo-Norman planned town. Its layout is preserved from the middle ages, and its ancient character is enhanced by a number of exceptionally fine buildings from the middle ages and the early modern period.

The Rock dominates the history of the town, just as it does its landscape. It was the citadel of the kings of Munster in the early middle ages and the name Cashel itself is a borrowing from the Latin *castellum*, a fortress. Unlike Tara of the Kings, Cashel of the Kings has no pagan associations whatsoever; not only is there nothing on the Rock that predates the arrival of Christianity in Ireland, but the earliest traditions surrounding the Rock all have a strong Christian element. St Patrick is recorded as having baptised one of the kings of Cashel, Oengus, and in the course of the ceremony to have inadvertently driven his staff into the foot of the king who muffled his scream thinking such a physical ordeal was part of the ritual! In fact, the Eoganachta, who were kings at

Cashel, c. 1900 (courtesy of French Gallery, Dublin)

Cashel through the early middle ages, actually claimed that Cashel was not always known to man but that it had been revealed in a vision to their fourth-century ancestor, Conal Corc.

If there is a single year in Cashel's history that might be picked out as pivotal it is 1101. In the closing years of the eleventh century there had begun a movement to bring the institution of the Irish church, which had been rather isolated in its practices, into line with the church elsewhere in Europe. The first of a number of synods at which the future of the Irish church was hammered out was held at Cashel in 1101, and the king of Munster, Muirchertach O'Brien, presided over it. He marked the occasion of the synod by giving the Rock itself to the church. No greater gesture could be imagined: the handing over of the ancient seat of secular power was the ultimate imprimatur, the ultimate seal of approval, on the movement to reform the Irish church. Central to the idea of reform was the establishment of dioceses.

Ten years after the synod of Cashel another synod, held at Rath Breasail, probably in Cork, decided on the make-up of the new dioceses and Cashel was made an archbishopric, second only to Armagh.

When the Anglo-Normans came to Cashel at the end of the twelfth century, at least three buildings were standing on the Rock: the round tower, Cormac's chapel and a cathedral. The latter was not the one we see now but its immediate predecessor, built about 1170 by Donal Mór O'Brien, a prolific church-builder in the region. Cormac's chapel was begun in 1127 and consecrated in 1134. It takes its name from its royal patron, Cormac McCarthy, and was evidently served by Benedictine monks who had come to Cashel from their monastery in Regensburg in southern Germany. Cormac's chapel is an astonishing work of architecture, the earliest and finest example in Ireland of the Romanesque style. It has been a centre of attention since its consecration, which was witnessed and celebrated by important clerics and noblemen, right through the middle ages, through the eighteenth century when Archbishop Bolton enthused about it to Dean Swift, suggesting the dean donate some money to help in its preservation, and through to today when it can claim to be internationally the best known medieval church in Ireland.

The Anglo-Normans were drawn to Cashel because of its political and ecclesiastical importance in the lives of their unwilling Gaelic hosts. Despite the disadvantages of not having a river running through it, Cashel was an obvious site for a colonial settlement: quite aside from the fact that land around it was exceptionally good, it was a central place, with roads, possibly quite ancient, running out of it in all directions; indeed, if one takes a map and draws a circle connecting Thurles, Killenaule, Fethard, Clonmel, Cahir and Tipperary, Cashel would more or less be in the centre.

The strategic merits of the Rock would hardly have been overlooked either. But rather than fortify it, the Normans honoured the promise made by the king of Munster in 1101 that the Rock would be a place of worship, and they had no difficulty in having Irish men serve there as archbishops.

Actually, bishops and archbishops of Irish birth were not averse to getting involved in the Norman colonisation of Ireland. They contributed to the founding of towns and the town of Cashel is a prime example of this.

Cashel had its genesis as a town in a charter granted by Archbishop Donatus O'Lonergan, an Irishman, in the year 1216. It was a new town: rather than develop slowly and organically from a smaller settlement, it was systematically laid out and built to a plan. This is not to say that there was no settlement on the site prior to the Normans. On the contrary, we know from contemporary sources that there was an 'old town' as well, and this may well have been the settlement founded by the king of Munster and his people after they relinquished control of the Rock to the church.

While the medieval origin of Cashel town does not impinge on the consciousness of, say, a car driver the way it does in Athlone or New Ross, where we tend to associate the word 'medieval' with impossibly narrow streets, it is nonetheless present. Imagine yourself coming into Cashel from the Dublin side. At the edge of town you pass a row of terraced properties on the right-hand side, and at the end of these you turn sharply to the right. Straight ahead of you is Main Street, the town's principal thoroughfare, leading on towards Cork, while running away to the left is Friar Street which brings you towards Clonmel. When you are at the junction of these two streets you are at the heart of the medieval town. John Street, at least as far as the Church of Ireland cathedral, and Moor Lane, leading northwards from Main Street, are also legacies of the medieval town. Main Street is split in two by a narrow row of properties, among them the small neo-classical town hall. These properties are built on what was originally the market square, probably the site of the shambles mentioned in a document in 1230. The name Main Street is not of medieval origin. In the fifteenth century this thoroughfare was referred to as the High Street, and in the following century it was known as St Nicholas Street.

All these streets are today lined with attractive two-or three-storey buildings, some with very good Georgian features. These properties, the buildings and their back yards, occupy the sites of the town's original medieval properties. In towns of medieval origin the plots tend not to change either shape or size, even if the buildings are replaced every century or two. Quirke's Castle, the four-storeyed battlemented tower-house which dominates the south side of Main Street and which is now a hotel, gives the best impression of the width of the street frontage of a medieval plot. This was built in the fifteenth century on the site of an earlier house. Some of the properties along Main Street and the other medieval streets have wider frontages today but this is the result of the amalgamation in recent centuries of two or three of the original plots.

A town like Cashel probably saw building activity going on fairly regularly in the middle ages. There was hardly a generation that was unfamiliar with the sound of stone masons' chisels or that did not see billowing clouds of white lime dust, or towering, rickety wooden scaffolding. For thirty years there was building activity going on up on the Rock as the Normans slowly replaced Donal O'Brien's old cathedral with a new Gothic building. While the archbishop had his cathedral on the Rock, a parish church was built in the town early in the thirteenth century to serve the pastoral needs of the townspeople. Dedicated to St John, it was located on John Street. Its site is now occupied by the Church of Ireland cathedral, built in the eighteenth century when the cathedral on the Rock was finally abandoned.

Also looking after the needs of the townspeople were two hospitals, both outside the town. The better known of the two was the hospital of St Nicholas, founded in the early thirteenth century and provided with fourteen beds and three chaplains. One of the thirteenth-century archbishops, David McKelly, made an unusual grant to this hospital of two flagons of ale out of every brewing made for sale within the limits of thirty messuages (properties) of the town. This grant was the subject of an interesting legal case half a century later when the Cistercians, a somewhat unpopular presence in thirteenth-century Cashel as will be seen below, had annexed the hospital to their own property and expected the supply of alcohol to be maintained. The town's 38 brewers had other ideas, but a jury ruled against them.

In common with many other Anglo-Norman towns in Ireland, Cashel would have been at the peak of its prosperity in the second half of the thirteenth century. It was around this time that Franciscans, Dominicans and Cistercians set up monastic houses in the vicinity of the urban area. The Dominicans, in 1243, and Franciscans, in 1265, built their monasteries right at the edge of the town but outside it. The enclosing walls of their foundations would have backed onto and overlooked the back gardens of the townspeople. The Dominican church, at the north end of the town, still survives, and it is notable today for its fine thirteenth- and fifteenth-century windows. But time has been unkind to the Franciscan friary and the present Catholic church occupies its site.

The Cistercians founded their establishment, Hore abbey, in 1272, in the open countryside to the west of the Rock. They owed their presence at Cashel to Archbishop David MacCarville, an Irishman who took the Cistercian habit in 1269. MacCarville claimed to have had a dream in which Benedictines conspired to cut off his head, and he duly replaced them with Cistercians from Mellifont abbey. MacCarville may have been right in thinking the Benedictines did not like him; he was certainly unpopular in other quarters: when, for example, he united the leper hospital of St Nicholas with his new Cistercian foundation, he allegedly emptied it of its inmates, and the Cistercians then demanded that the townspeople pay the same duty to them as they had been paying to the leper hospital, which was greatly resented. Local Cashel people of English origin also complained that the Irish in the Cistercian community were responsible for murder and pillage.

This sort of racial tension was a signpost to the future. Records of the fourteenth century in Ireland are dominated by accounts of war between the Irish and the Anglo-Normans or, as we can begin to call them at this stage, English. Towns responded to this endemic warfare by erecting walls. Twice in the early 1300s provision was made for the walling of Cashel, and the area that was walled was about 30 acres, with the wall running around the town for a length of almost a mile. It is possible today to trace the outline of this protective structure, although it does involve the physical effort of going along the backs of some of the properties in the town. Fortunately, the most accessible parts of the walls (behind the Bolton Library) are clearly indicated as such for visitors. There are also hints in the historical sources of suburbs, streets outside the walled area, but nothing is known of them.

There were at least five gates protecting the town entrances. All are gone but we can locate where they were with a fair degree of accuracy. The Canopy Gate, also known as the Upper Gate, was located at the east end or Dublin end of Main Street. At the far end of Main Street was St Nicholas' Gate, or Lower Gate, around where the post office is today. A third gate was Moor Gate, close to the Dominican friary. Friar Gate was on Friar Street, close to where the Presentation convent is today. Finally, there was John's Gate, on John Street, close to the present Church of Ireland cathedral.

The one medieval building in the town which survives from the period after the walls were erected is Quirke's Castle, the tower-house on Main Street. This is a fairly typical fortified residence of the fifteenth century, rather like the towers that dot the Tipperary countryside. Its position facing onto what was the market square suggests that its owner might have been involved in the town's commerce. One of the archbishops built a similar tower onto the west end of the cathedral on the Rock.

Most of the activity in Cashel in the late middle ages – the fourteenth, fifteenth and sixteenth centuries – seems to revolve around the Rock and its archbishops. One event in this period that has had positive repercussions for the town's present tourist profile was the building on the Rock of the hall of the vicars choral, a residence for the minor clerics and laymen who assisted in the chanting in the cathedral. The visit of the earl of Kildare was less positive. His legacy to the Rock was a smouldering cathedral; the archbishop had been complaining to Henry VII about the earl who responded by setting fire to the great church, and he justified his action to the king saying he incinerated the building because he thought the archbishop was in there at the time!

Worse was to face Cashel. The town got off to a good start in the seventeenth century with Charles I giving it a charter, elevating it to the status of a city, but James II reversed this. In 1647 Lord Inchiquin and the parliamentary forces marched on the town. The townspeople retreated with their forces to the Rock, but Inchiquin took it by storm, perpetrating unspeakable atrocities on the garrison and townspeople holed up there. Cashel was one of many towns left devastated by the parliamentary forces in the seventeenth century. A letter written at that time paints a tragic picture of a town that had been destroyed by fire in a matter of hours. The picture is all the more tragic for the gloating with which the correspondent reports that the few well-built stone houses of English people in the town had withstood the inferno.

Cashel had a more prosperous eighteenth century, kick-started by William of Orange, who, right at the end of the seventeenth century, restored its city status in recognition of the kindness its townspeople had shown to his soldiers who had been injured at the siege of Limerick. As a city, Cashel had a corporation composed of mayor, aldermen, bailiffs and other officials. The corporation elected members to parliament until the borough lost its franchise in the 1800s. Incidentally, after the act of union, Cashel's parliamentary representation was reduced from two to one, and from 1809 to 1812 its one seat was held by Robert Peel, later Sir Robert, the English prime minister. Robert's father was a wealthy English industrialist, and he bought the seat for his son who had just graduated from Oxford.

By the eighteenth century the town walls had become redundant. In 1704 Alderman Thomas Chardwick was allowed make a doorway eight feet wide through the town wall into his garden. The repair of properties destroyed in the wars required stone and the townspeople saw the Rock as a great facility and eagerly quarried away until an alarmed dean and chapter of the cathedral put a stop to it. Cashel cathedral, which had become Protestant in the sixteenth century, was abandoned during the 1700s, and the archbishops had a new cathedral erected for themselves in the town on the site of the old medieval parish church. In deserting the cathedral on the Rock they unfortunately stripped the roof, leaving the building open to the elements. The first Church of Ireland cathedral in the town was replaced in 1783 by the present neo-classical building. The Catholic church on Friar Street is a little younger, built about 1800, and it too is neo-classical.

The outstanding building of the eighteenth century in Cashel is the palace of the Protestant archbishops located on the north side of Main Street. This was designed by Sir Edward Lovett Pearce, best known as the architect of the parliament house in Dublin, and the first archbishop to take up residence in it was Theophilus Bolton. He was quite a bibliophile, and had his own library attached to the house by a passage. This was designed perhaps with one eye on the famous Marsh's Library in Dublin, also located beside an archiepiscopal palace. Bolton's extraordinary collection was bequeathed in 1744 to the clergy of the diocese, and was moved a century later to its present building in the grounds of the Church of Ireland cathedral.

In addition to the palace and the cathedral, high-quality Georgian houses were built around the town, particularly along John Street, and a charter school was built at the edge of the town, but this is now sadly demolished. All this suggests prosperity in certain quarters, much of it sponsored by the established church. The Catholic church made rather less of a contribution, partly because it decided to relinquish Cashel as a diocesan centre and moved to Thurles instead. Despite the indications of wealth, visitors to the town in the late 1700s and 1800s, among them Archibald Stark, described Cashel as impoverished. Around the middle of the nineteenth century the very high proportions of vacant houses on the one hand, and of households with a female rather than a male head on the other, indicate a degree of urban poverty which, incidentally, can be paralleled in other Tipperary towns at the same time.

Cashel's distance from a river was never to its advantage, and once the railways appeared and by-passed Cashel, the town was always likely to struggle against well-served places like Thurles. It is ironic, perhaps, that a town so near to Charles Bianconi's Longfield House should have transportation problems. By the end of the nineteenth century the markets held on Wednesdays and Saturdays were dwindling, and the mills along the River Suir, a couple of miles to the west, were no longer yielding big profits. The local clergy was blaming this on the lack of a railway.

Despite the picture of economic gloom, the nineteenth century saw improvements in the quality of life for at least some Cashel townspeople with the erection of the courthouse and prison, a small Methodist church, a Presentation convent and a few schools. The town commissioners, an administrative body set up just before the famine after the corporation had been dissolved by an act of parliament, provided the infrastructure which was to bring the town into the twentieth century. They built the gasworks which provided the town with its first proper street lighting. They also took responsibility for street paving. Best of all, the commissioners solved the town's chronic water problem by piping water from an out-of-town reservoir. Five fountains for public use were placed in the centre of the town, and these can be seen today, thankfully restored, behind the town hall in Main Street. Water was also piped into houses for a small fee. Also, late nineteenth-century Cashel had quite a diversified retail structure, with everything from drapers to coal merchants to pawnbrokers. No less than eight cattle dealers illustrate the importance of pastoral farming to the town's economy.

The twentieth century, at least up to the 1960s, saw only small changes to this commercial profile. The replacement of services was more substantial, particularly the use of electricity instead of gas. One major change in this century, especially in fairly recent years, is tourism. In the 1800s the glorious ruins on the Rock began a rapid decay. The archbishops of the established church recognised the great historical and cultural value of those ruins, and looked after them as best they could. At the end of the century they passed into state care, and maintenance and repair work has been going on ever since. The arrival of motorised transport not only expanded the town's hinterland but also made the Rock more accessible, and today it contributes invaluably to the town's prosperity.

The awareness of the value of heritage has mushroomed in recent years, leaving Cashel and towns like it with the challenge of achieving a balance between two conflicting forces, the needs of the future on the one hand, and the legacy of the past on the other. It is a challenge the town has faced with good results so far, as any visitor will testify. The town continues to evolve but in a way and at a pace that will only be obvious with the passage of time. It will be interesting to hear what a Thomas Davis lecturer will have to say about Cashel in a hundred years from now.

Select bibliography
S. Lewis: *A Topographical Dictionary of Ireland*, London, 1837, i, pp. 284-8
J. D. White: *Cashel of the Kings, Being a History of the City of Cashel*, second edition, Cashel, 1876
J. Gleeson: *Cashel of the Kings*, Dublin, 1927
J. Bradley: 'The medieval towns of Tipperary', in W. Nolan (ed.), *Tipperary: History and Society*, Dublin, 1985, pp. 42-5
A. Thomas: *The Walled Towns of Ireland*, Dublin, 1992, ii, pp. 46-8

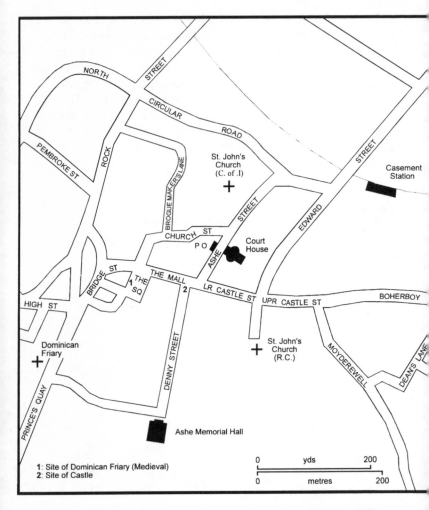

Tralee, based on Ordnance Survey Road Atlas of Ireland, 1985

TRALEE

John Bradley

The pale moon was rising above the green mountain,
The sun was declining beneath the blue sea,
When I strayed with my love to the pure crystal fountain,
That stands in the beautiful vale of Tralee.

THESE words, more than any others, have made the name of
Tralee known throughout Ireland and wherever the Irish
have settled abroad. In this ballad William Pembroke
Mulchinock immortalised his love for Mary O'Connor. 'She
was,' he tells us, 'lovely and fair as the rose of summer, yet
'twas not her beauty alone that won me. Oh no, 'twas the
truth in her eyes ever dawning that made me love Mary, the
Rose of Tralee'. They were, in the best (or perhaps the worst)
traditions of romance, a pair of star-crossed lovers. He came
from a rich and landed family. She was a poor servant girl.
In the claustrophobic social world of Victorian Ireland such a
marriage was impossible. When the family discovered the
depth of the relationship they packed him off, out of the
country. By the time he returned Mary had died of consumption, that deadly nineteenth-century malady without
whose fatal interceptions one is at times tempted to speculate that romantic love itself might well have perished.

The song, however, presents us with none of this trag-
edy. It concentrates instead on the moments of happiness
when the lovers first met and it was this cheerful mood
which stimulated the holding of the first Rose of Tralee
festival in 1959. Since then the festival has become the largest
in Ireland. In 1992 it attracted entrants from 32 centres in
nine different countries. 100,000 visitors came to Tralee in
the course of the festival week. Its climax, the selection of the
Rose, was relayed on television to millions of viewers at
home and abroad. Financially it generated a revenue of over
fourteen and a half million pounds for the town. All in all, it
is an impressive annual tally to accrue from the glimpse of

Tralee from the air (Cambridge Aerial Photographs)

truth in the eyes of a lover.

The modern visitor to Tralee sees a town which, in several aspects, would have been familiar to the first Rose. For although Tralee has many modern buildings the architectural character of the town is essentially a nineteenth-century one. Castle Street and the Mall are flanked by tightly-packed, three- and four-storeyed, Victorian houses standing in serried file; Day Place and Denny Street, characterised by their neat iron railings and elegant fan-light doorways, are more spacious and were clearly developed to provide accommodation for Tralee's rising professional class; the main public buildings, the courthouse, churches, schools, hospital, and civic offices, are located some distance behind the main thoroughfares where they were removed from the hustle and bustle that would have been associated with market day. At the outskirts, the solidity of the Victorian structures fades into a ribbon of low-rise buildings, single-storey houses and bungalows which are the first feature to greet the visitor on the approach roads to the town. The core of Tralee, however, still retains the sober character of a Victorian market town and its streetscape is a visible reminder of the urban expansion and confidence of nineteenth-century Ireland which did so much to mould the physical appearance of our towns.

Nonetheless, the visitor who thought that this was all there was to Tralee would be very much mistaken. For behind the facade lies the story of a much more ancient town. The impact of the nineteenth-century builders has been so great that it is easy to forget that Tralee was for long the medieval capital of west Munster and that it has an ancestry going back almost 800 years.

It was the Normans who were responsible for the foundation of Tralee. By 1197 the city of Limerick, peacefully it seems, had accepted an Anglo-Norman governor and in the years that followed the Anglo-Norman adventurers pushed westwards into County Limerick and north Kerry. We know very little about the progress of this invasion but the most important thrust, from a Kerry point of view, occurred in 1214 and 1215 when, taking advantage of internal strife among the MacCarthys, the Anglo-Normans under Meiler FitzHenry built a chain of fortresses along the River Maine and also a castle at Killorglin. The effect of this manoeuvre was that it enabled colonists to settle in the fertile lowlands of north Kerry and the Dingle peninsula.

We cannot be certain what it was that attracted the first Anglo-Normans to the site of the future town. The physical beauty of the setting may have been a factor. It is nestled under the protecting flank of the Slieve Mish mountains, in the vale of the River Lee (Mulchinock's 'pure crystal fountain') at the point where it enters Tralee Bay. The place-name gives us a clue to one feature which attracted the first settlers. Trá Lí, 'the strand of the river Lee', suggests that the site may have been important as a harbour or landing place in the early years of the Anglo-Norman invasion. The other feature which attracted them to Tralee was, undoubtedly, the existence of the nearby monastery of Ratass. In the twelfth century Ratass was a prominent ecclesiastical centre, second in the county only to Ardfert. Indeed there was a rivalry between the two because Ratass functioned for a number of years as the episcopal see of Kerry. Ratass today is a vast cemetery but the early ogham stone and cross-slab, and most of all the remains of the ancient church, rebuilt in Romanesque style, are visible reminders of its importance in the twelfth century. The Anglo-Normans came to Tralee, one is tempted to say, because the roads led to Ratass. Ratass, however, had limited potential for development. The nearby harbour was preferred and so the town was founded a little under a mile to the west beside the sea. The topography of Tralee has changed greatly since the twelfth century. Over the years, the River Lee and the Gyle or Big River, on which the town is actually situated, have deposited great quantities of silt. The ancient harbour has been filled up and the sea is now the best part of two miles from the town.

Little is known about the early history of Tralee. Its founder was probably John FitzThomas, one of the first of that branch of the FitzGeralds who were to become famous in Irish history as earls of Desmond. If we were to pinpoint a year of foundation then the town was probably established in 1216 or shortly thereafter. In that year John FitzThomas was granted most of north Kerry and, almost certainly, he began to develop the area fairly quickly. In establishing a town, he had to make three important provisions, otherwise prospective colonists would not take the risk of coming. Firstly the settlement had to be secure; secondly it had to have a market place; and thirdly, the founder had to provide for the spiritual welfare of the citizens by building a church.

The initial feature constructed on the site was probably the castle. This stood at the junction of Denny Street and Castle Street and was demolished in 1826 in order to make way for the construction of Denny Street. Originally it may have been an earthen fortification but, if so, it was not long before it was rebuilt with stone. Our evidence for it comes totally from late medieval sources when it functioned as one of the principal castles of the earls of Desmond. It is invariably referred to as the 'great castle of Tralee'.

The castle would have given a measure of security to the

new settlement but the settlers were primarily interested in the opportunity of making a living for themselves. The town had to have a market place where the produce of the surrounding countryside could be exposed for sale and where commodities from outside such as salt, fine clothes and wine could be purchased. We know that the main street of medieval Tralee was called 'Burgess Street', but it is not possible to identify its modern equivalent although High Street is perhaps the best candidate. Other streets which are mentioned in late medieval sources include 'Great Castle Street' and the 'Street of the New Manor', perhaps to be identified with Bridge Street and Castle Street respectively. In common with other Anglo-Norman towns it is to be expected that the houses occupied the street frontage of the long narrow plot that was given to each settler on arrival in the town. We can only speculate on what the first houses looked like.

Archaeological excavations in Wexford have shown that the initial Anglo-Norman structures there were built of post-and-wattle and were little different from the native houses which preceded them. We shall have to await the results of archaeological excavations in Tralee to discover if this was also the case in Kerry. Later in the middle ages we know that both timber-framed and stone houses of the tower house variety were present in the town. The market place itself was embellished with a cross and it was here in 1641 that the unfortunate jailer of Tralee was hanged.

A characteristic feature of all Anglo-Norman towns in Ireland is the presence of a single parish church and Tralee is no exception. The dedication was to St John and it has been speculated that it was originally in the charge of the knights hospitallers. Unfortunately the documentation is unclear on this matter. The surviving building, on Ashe Street, has the appearance of being a nineteenth-century structure but in fact substantial sections of an earlier building, perhaps of medieval date, are incorporated into the present edifice. Inside is an attractive font on a drum-shaped shaft with a barley-sugar twist, dated to 1623.

The harbour was clearly an important feature from early

times and it continued to function until the seventeenth century. A ship moored in the harbour of Tralee is referred to in 1612, and in 1628 a Hamburg ship of 120 tons was captured when it came into Tralee harbour with a cargo of pipestaves, timber and tar. By 1682, however, the harbour seems to have gone out of use and an account of that year states that it was only resorted to in bad weather. The silting up of the harbour was undoubtedly a major factor in its decline and the port of Tralee was moved to Blennerville where in the years following the great famine it became the principal port of emigration in the south-west.

An early indication of the growth of Tralee during its initial years is provided by the foundation of the Dominican friary in 1243. It was established by John FitzThomas Fitz-Gerald who was buried there in 1261 together with his son Maurice after their deaths at the battle of Callan. The friars were mendicants and their presence indicates that by 1243 the population of Tralee was large enough to support them as well as the regular clergy. The friary became one of the principal burial places of the earls of Desmond and it was here that the first and eighth earls, among others, were interred. The precise date of the friary's suppression is not known but it could hardly have functioned later than 1580 when the lord justice, Sir William Pelham, garrisoned it with 300 footmen and a company of horses. A number of architectural fragments still survive in the garden of the present Dominican friary and these include portions of the cloister arcade. Built into the wall of St John's Catholic church is an attractive fifteenth-century stone panel showing the assumption of the Blessed Virgin. From these fragments it is clear that the friary was rebuilt in the fifteenth century. It is known to have consisted of an extensive complex of buildings, located in the vicinity of the square, which was removed during the Cromwellian period to supply building stone for the townspeople.

Another indication of the prosperity of the town during the thirteenth century is provided by a murage grant of 1286 which enabled Thomas FitzMaurice, lord of Desmond, to levy a tax for seven years in order to build a wall around

Tralee. Unfortunately we have no idea as to the course of the town defences but again this is something which archaeological investigations should reveal in the future.

The town almost certainly had a corporation from an early date but the first evidence for its existence occurs in 1298. In that year the burgage rent, paid by the townspeople, amounted to 100 shillings suggesting that there were 100 burgages within the town. In turn this would suggest a population of between 600 and 1,000 people.

Records of Tralee in the later middle ages are few and far between. In 1346 Maurice FitzDavid and William Stakepoll were appointed custodians of the vill while in 1375, Henry Peverell, a merchant of Bristol, tells us that he was robbed of goods to the value of 100 marks in Tralee. Throughout this time the town remained in the hands of the earls of Desmond and the upheavals caused in the sixteenth century by the struggle between the earls and the Dublin government had a major impact on Tralee. The government officials resented the great power of the Desmonds and did everything that they could to curb it. The Desmonds, on their part, were not unaware of the government's stealthy intentions. The earls corresponded with continental powers and the landings of French troops in 1570 and of Spanish forces in 1579 reinforced the government's mistrust. By a series of intimidations and threats, as well as the somewhat injudicious murder of two government officials in Tralee castle, Gerald, the fifteenth earl, was forced into rebellion. He adopted a scorched-earth policy and one of his first actions, in 1580, was to burn Tralee to prevent it from falling into the hands of the government forces. Sir William Pelham tells us that on his arrival he found 'all the houses at Tralee burnt and the castles razed, saving only the abbey'. In the three years that followed the government took advantage of its opportunity. The rich agricultural land of Munster was devastated and turned into a 'trembling sod'. Finally in 1583 the earl himself was betrayed, captured and beheaded.

The defeat and death of the earl led to the establishment of an English administration in Tralee and one of the first results of this was the preparation in 1584 of a survey of

Desmond property. This provides valuable information on Tralee and on the devastation caused in 1580. In the document it is described as:

> a certain large town or village called Tralee, which was formerly a well-inhabited borough, with a castle and edifices in it, formerly well and fully repaired, but now ruined and broken.

Almost all of the burgages and tenements are described as 'prostrated', 'waste' or 'broken'.

In the plantation of Munster which followed, Tralee was granted in 1587 to Edward Denny but any attempts at reconstruction were soon interrupted. In 1598, during the rebellion of the 'súgán' earl of Desmond, the town was abandoned by the English settlers and garrison. In 1600, however, Tralee was reoccupied by crown forces under Sir George Carew and in the same year the government drew up proposals to build a new town at Tralee and to make it into the county town of Kerry.

The Dennys were the family largely responsible for the rebuilding of Tralee in the early seventeenth century. In 1612 Arthur Denny received government approval to wall the town, although he never seems to have completed this project. In 1613 the town was granted a new charter of incorporation by James I which, as well as regulating the functioning of the corporation, also granted a weekly market and an annual fair. This grant was a clear sign of Denny's intention to import English colonists from whom profitable rents could be extracted. By 1622, 32 new English households had been established. The wars of the seventeenth century, however, were to prove destructive for Tralee; so much so, indeed, that they obliterated the town's medieval plan. It was burned by confederate forces in 1642, it suffered badly during the Cromwellian occupation of the 1650s, and in 1691 it was again burned, this time by Jacobite forces who wished to prevent it from falling into Williamite hands.

In contrast, the eighteenth and nineteenth centuries were periods of stability and prosperity, resulting, in particular, from the opening up of the port at Blennerville through which large quantities of grain and butter were exported. It was a prosperity which we still find reflected in the architectural fabric of the present town and some of Tralee's most distinctive buildings date from this time. The courthouse for instance, with its imposing Ionic portico designed by William Vitruvius Morrison, was built in 1835 at a cost of £14,000. St John's Catholic church in Castle Street was constructed between 1854 and 1870 by the distinguished Gothic revival architect J. J. McCarthy. The Dominican church, also in Gothic style, was erected between 1867 and 1871 to designs by Edward Welby Pugin, the father of the Gothic revival, and George Ashlin.

In this century, too, Tralee has continued to prosper and its success is reflected in buildings such as Revington's Department Store (now Ryle and Nolan's) on the Mall and the Ashe Hall, surely one of the most attractive county buildings in Ireland, which was constructed in 1928 to the award-winning designs of Thomas Cullen. In recent years, largely due to the foresight and energy of Tralee urban district council, FÁS and Shannon Development, a number of important attractions have been added to the town. Siamsa Tíre, the national folk theatre of Ireland, founded in 1974 as a showpiece of Irish music, mime and dance, opened its purpose-built theatre, modelled on Staigue fort, in 1991. The Ashe Hall now houses Kerry County Museum where there is a permanent display of life in the county from pre-history to the present as well as 'Geraldine Tralee', an imaginative reconstruction of daily life in a medieval Irish town through which the visitor is conducted in specially-built electric cars. A section of the Tralee and Dingle railway, originally opened in 1891, has been rebuilt and passengers can now travel between Tralee and Blennerville. At Blennerville itself the windmill, the largest working windmill in these islands, was restored and reopened in 1992. A waterworld has been constructed adjoining the steam railway station at Ballard and plans are being prepared for the full reconstruction of the emigrant ship *Jeanie Johnston* at Blennerville.

I began this essay with an account of a man and a woman in a garden and perhaps I may be forgiven for concluding it with revelations. My revelation is a simple one. It is that the past is, in one way or another, the engine which drives the future. Whether in the economic sphere, in terms of creating attractions for the heritage industry, or philosophic in terms of providing people with opinions, expectations, a social ethos and values, the past is seamlessly interwoven with the present. Most important, however, is the psychological boost, one might almost say the creative energy, which the contemplation of the past can generate. We live in a time of economic recession and of high unemployment. It is easy to be dispirited, to be downhearted, to think that nothing can change. But the contemplation of Tralee's past shows us that it is not a linear story. There have been enormous changes. Tralee has faced severe challenges in the past yet the town has not only survived, it has prospered. It has done so, I believe, because of the strength of its community, a strength based on tradition (a shared past) and innovation (the constant search for the best possible future for the community and its children). Reflection on the past need not be introspective, as it is often popularly seen to be, it can also stimulate the inventiveness, courage and resilience to tackle whatever the future may hold. By pioneering projects of local reconstruction and development, by becoming a tourist destination in its own right, and by fostering the image that vitality is a birthright, Tralee has not only reclaimed its past, it has also guaranteed its future.

Select bibliography
A. B. Rowan [pseudonym 'X']: 'The antiquities of Tralee', *Kerry Magazine*, i (1854), pp. 2-180
M. A. Hickson: 'Notes on Kerry topography, ancient and modern', *Journal of the Royal Society of Antiquaries of Ireland*, xv (1879) - xix (1889)
T. J. Barrington: *Discovering Kerry*, Dublin, 1976
J. Bradley: 'The medieval towns of Kerry', *North Munster Antiquarian Journal*, xxviii (1986), pp. 28-39
J. Bradley: *Geraldine Tralee*, Tralee, 1991
M. O'Dwyer: *Tralee: A Historical Guide*, Tralee, 1991

YOUGHAL

A . F. O'Brien

YOUGHAL, County Cork, is an old market town, seaside resort and, formerly, a fishing port which lies on the western shore of the Blackwater estuary some 30 miles east of Cork city, 48 miles south-west of Waterford, 17 miles east of Midleton, 18 miles south of Lismore and 19 miles south-west of Dungarvan. Other towns in its region are Castlemartyr, Tallow and Cappoquin. The town is situated on the western shore of Youghal harbour which is enclosed between two hills. One of these hills, called Knockaverry, rises immediately over the town. At this point, the channel is about half a mile in breadth and here the River Tourig, the boundary between Counties Cork and Waterford, and the River Black-water enter Youghal Bay. A. R. Orme in his geographical survey of Youghal has pointed out that 'the choice of site for a settlement which could serve both as a fortress controlling the river mouth and as a seaport exploiting the commercial potential of the hinterland was strictly limited'.

Youghal developed on virtually the only site suited to the needs and resources of the Anglo-Norman invaders. Both the development and topography of the town and indeed the long-term importance of its port were therefore shaped essentially by the morphology of its situation. That observation, however, should not lead us to minimise the importance of man in promoting or retarding the fortunes of the town in the course of history.

Youghal is the principal town of the barony of Imokilly, on the eastern border of which it lies. The borough of Youghal was the most important of the three boroughs of the medieval manor of Inchiquin which comprised much of east County Cork. The other two boroughs were Inchiquin and Kinsalebeg. These three boroughs were baronial boroughs established by the lord of the manor of Inchiquin essentially for military and strategic purposes. As such, Youghal was

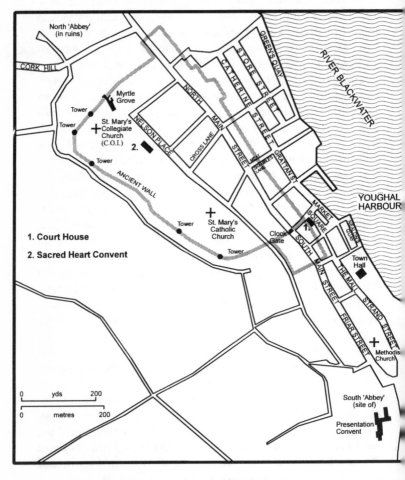

Youghal, based on Ordnance Survey of Ireland, six inches to one mile, 1935

primarily an agent and instrument of Anglo-Norman colonisation in Ireland. For the lord of the manor, of which it was an important component, that military, colonial function transcended in importance the economic and commercial role of the town.

However, in course of time, Youghal became a seaport town with an active commerce of considerable importance, and it continued to be such from later medieval times until comparatively recently. In 1845, for example, the town was described as 'a post and market town, a seaport, a parliamentary borough, and the practical capital of the south-eastern district of the county of Cork'. Indeed, so important was Youghal politically, militarily and commercially in the late sixteenth and seventeenth centuries that the English government proposed to create a new county of Youghal of which Youghal would be the county town. In the event, that proposal came to nothing and was successfully resisted by Lord Broghill, son of Richard Boyle, the first earl of Cork.

Historically, therefore, the town of Youghal was strategically and militarily important. From the time of its capture by the English it was garrisoned by crown forces, quartered, first, in a fort fronting the waterside at the eastern end of the town and, later, in a barracks located near the present Cork Hill. In the course of the nineteenth century, however, the Youghal garrison was run down in favour of that established in the new military barracks at Fermoy. Youghal, therefore, played a major role in some of the crucial political developments affecting both its own region and Ireland as a whole.

Some kind of Viking settlement, perhaps a proto-town, appears to have existed in the neighbourhood of Youghal, but the town is essentially thirteenth-century in origin. The real founder of Youghal was Maurice fitz Gerald II, the second baron of Offaly, who obtained possession of his father's lands, including Imokilly, in 1215. He colonised the town with citizens of Bristol and settlers from other parts of England, especially south-west England, and Wales. In the course of the thirteenth century, Youghal witnessed a considerable and rapid development as a centre of settlement and trade. Furthermore, it acquired borough status by way

181

Youghal c. 1587, redrawn by A. R. Orme from Pacata Hibernia, *London,*
1633

of a basic charter of liberties, privileges and immunities con-
ferred on it by its lord, the lord of Inchiquin. By the late
thirteenth century Youghal had a weekly market and a
yearly fair. A subsequent charter, that of 1609, increased this
to two markets and two fairs. The establishment of the yearly fair, in the course of the thirteenth century, testifies
strongly to the economic importance of Youghal. Already, it
was engaged in trade with Wales, south-west England and
parts of continental Europe, notably Bordeaux. Subsequently, for political and economic reasons, overseas trade contracted, but there was a marked revival in the course of the
later fifteenth and early sixteenth centuries, by which time
the area of maritime trade had expanded to include Spain
and Portugal. In south-west England alone, in addition to
the major port of Bristol, Youghal traded extensively with a
cluster of ports in Devon, Cornwall, Somerset and Dorset.
These included Bridgwater, Minehead, Ilfracombe, Barn-

staple, Padstow, St Ives, Fowey, Plymouth, Dartmouth and Poole. Youghal's principal exports were fish and hides while cloth, cereals and manufactured goods were imported from England and wine from Spain, Portugal and south-west France. Indeed, by the early sixteenth century Youghal was an entrepot port, exporting Portuguese spices to England. Once again, Youghal was a vibrant seaport trading town.

By the later thirteenth century, it was linked to a number of inland towns and markets. This whole network of towns and markets formed an important commercial infrastructure. As a port town, Youghal was a major component of this network.

By the late thirteenth century too, the commercial and physical growth of the town, notwithstanding the limitations imposed on it by the physical constraints of its location, was already impressive. For example, the burgesses of Youghal held four water mills, while the town was serviced by a ferry which traversed the Blackwater. The ownership of that ferry ultimately became a possession of the corporation of Youghal. In 1830, a bridge was erected over the Blackwater north-east of the town linking Foxhole, in the parish of St Mary, Youghal, to the parish of Clashmore, County Waterford. The builders of this bridge were obliged to compensate the corporation for the loss of the profits of the ferry. In 1288, the profits accruing from the ferry were estimated to be worth two pounds yearly. Indeed, at that time, the profits which the town of Youghal produced for its owner, the lord of Inchiquin, amounted to nearly 61 per cent of all the revenues of the manor of Inchiquin, of which Youghal was a component.

Youghal was a walled town and, although these walls have been considerably restored over the years while other sections have been demolished or breached in the course of the post-medieval expansion of the town, a substantial part of the original wall remains. The surviving section of the wall dates to the thirteenth century, but there are some seventeenth-century additions.

In order to provide capital for the building of the town walls, grants, called murage grants, which permitted the town to impose levies on goods traded within the town, were made to Youghal by the English crown in 1275 and 1357 and further grants were made in the late fourteenth and fifteenth centuries. However, in practice, the proceeds of murage grants could be allocated to purposes other than wall building. It did not necessarily follow, therefore, that grants of murage were followed by the repair, reinforcement or building of town walls. As much as a defensive structure, the town wall represented in a very physical way the limits of urban freedom, marking off the town from its feudalised surroundings.

The surviving town walls of Youghal have been described as 'possibly the best-preserved medieval town walls in Ireland'. The surviving portion of the wall consists of the western and north-western sections extending from the south-west of the medieval town to the west and north of St Mary's collegiate church. This church, which is situated within the line of the town wall in the north-west corner of the old town, was built about 1250 on the site of an older edifice, the remains of the older church, which can still be seen, being incorporated in the new building. The thirteenth-century church was restored and extended in the fourteenth century, and further changes were made in 1468 when Thomas, eighth earl of Desmond, built a new chancel and east window. The tower, which is such a notable feature of the church, is of thirteenth-century origin but was subsequently strengthened, perhaps in the fifteenth century. St Mary's is now the Church of Ireland parish church of the parish of St Mary's, Youghal.

Close to St Mary's church to the south-east is the College of Our Lady of Youghal, founded by Thomas, eighth earl of Desmond, in 1464 for a warden, eight ordained fellows and eight lay brothers. The college was acquired by the English adventurer, Sir Walter Raleigh, who subsequently sold it, with other plantation properties, to Richard Boyle, another adventurer and later the first earl of Cork, who was a major figure in the English conquest and colonisation of Ireland in the late sixteenth and early seventeenth centuries. Boyle then proceeded to take over the endowments of the college. On the site of the college is New College House built in 1781-2. It was formerly the property of the duke of Devonshire, who, in 1753, succeeded the Boyle family in Youghal and elsewhere in Munster. The building is now the Sacred Heart convent.

To the north-east of St Mary's church and north of the college lies the house now known as Myrtle Grove. This was originally the residence of the warden of the college and dates from the middle of the fifteenth century. In the course of the plantation settlement, the warden's residence came into possession of Raleigh, around whose ownership a colourful but often inaccurate mythology has developed. Boyle acquired it from Raleigh in 1602, and in 1616 he disposed of it to Sir Laurence Parsons. The residence is now a much-altered Elizabethan house. This complex of buildings occupies the entire north-western section of the medieval town which is the core and heart of modern Youghal.

Although the south wall of the medieval town has largely disappeared, the base of some of it at least seems to have survived in the form of a pathway rising westwards at an angle of 20-30 degrees towards the top of the plateau and extending from the Clock Gate to the remains of one of the defensive towers situated at the junction of the western and southern sections of the wall. At the top of the plateau, the present roadway incorporates the old road to Cork. This plateau restricted the expansion of the town to the west until modern times. Even today, there is relatively little development here, largely because the expansion of Youghal in the eighteenth and nineteenth centuries has been mainly to the east, south and south-west along the line of the modern road to Cork. Much of such development as there has been to the west of the medieval town, along the plateau, consists of local authority housing.

The medieval town was particularly vulnerable on its western side and here the wall, with its defensive towers, was especially important. From this roadway, on the western side of the town, and of course from the western wall itself, there is a commanding view over the old town to the harbour and estuary below. Indeed, in 1642 during the siege of

Youghal which followed the outbreak of the Irish rebellion in 1641, Richard Boyle, earl of Cork, who defended the town in the Protestant and English interest, refortified part of the west wall behind St Mary's church and mounted cannon there to harass enemy shipping threatening the harbour or trying to land troops in Youghal.

The Clock Gate, which is one of the most distinctive features of Youghal, is situated at the junction of the present North and South Main Streets. It stands on the site of Trinity Castle close to the Iron Gate. This was the south gate of the medieval town of Youghal. Trinity Castle had begun to deteriorate by 1772 when it was proposed to take it down. It was demolished in 1776-7 and in its place was built the present Clock Tower to the design of the architect William Meade and to the specifications of the corporation of Youghal.

The medieval quays lay immediately east of the present Main Street. Anthony Orme has pointed out that owing to the restrictions on development westwards, the town expanded riverwards by means of comparatively limited slob reclamation so that, by the close of the medieval period, the riverside walls lay 40-60 yards east of Main Street and a walled suburb, the so-called Base Town, with an adjacent quay had become attached to the south-east wall of the old town. The location and function of the Base Town have been described by Orme as follows: 'South of the twin-towered Trinity Castle the Base Town probably functioned as the warehousing sector for the adjoining quays, access to which was provided by the Water Gate, and also housed fishermen and others engaged in the port's activities. The east wall ran along the water's edge but, by the close of the sixteenth century, additional quays had been built beyond the walls north of the main harbour.' The Water Gate, it should be observed, was 'restored' in the nineteenth century, a time of considerable expansion on the slob lands to the east of the town.

In 1607 the town of Youghal consisted of a principal street about a mile long, the upper part extending north and the Base Town south with a few outlets. By 1681, the town evidently had not changed significantly; it was described as consisting of 'one fair street continued from gate to gate'. Youghal in the late sixteenth and early seventeenth centuries has been described by Orme as follows: 'the principal built-up area lay along both sides of the present [North] Main Street and Church Street and consisted largely of small, steeply gabled, two-storeyed dwellings interspersed with some larger castellated town houses and a few buildings fronted by Dutch gables, reflecting Youghal's prosperity and trading contacts. From the vicinity of the church and Myrtle Grove ... a further road, now represented by Emmet Place and Ashe Street, ran south-east through orchards and vege-table gardens roughly parallel to Main Street with which it connected through Cross and Chapel Lanes.' This area comprised most of medieval Youghal.

Apart from those already described, the important or interesting buildings in this part of the town are either on, or adjacent to, the North Main Street. Some of these can be briefly described. On the west side of the street are the Red House, which is a brick building with Dutch renaissance details, which was built for the Uniacke family by a Dutch builder named Leuventhen in the period 1706-15, and the alms houses built in 1634 by Richard Boyle, first earl of Cork. In addition, there are the remnants of the Benedictine priory and also the later but defunct Campbell's Hotel. The Benedictine priory of St John the Evangelist was established in Youghal, apparently in the mid-fourteenth century, as a dependency of the priory of St John the Evangelist, Water-ford. During Cromwell's stay in Youghal, the priory was used to store supplies for his troops. This tradition of dese-cration has been strongly maintained and recently the building was used for commercial purposes, incongruously housing a video shop.

Campbell's Hotel, now MacCarthy's public house, was the principal hotel in Youghal before the establishment of the Devonshire Arms, the building of which formed part of the town's development to the south. At the rear of Campbell's Hotel, there was a theatre much used in the early nineteenth century by players drawn from the military garrison. The garrison contributed significantly to the social life of Youghal at that time. For example, in summertime military bands entertained the strolling citizenry by playing on the newly established Mall.

The east side of North Main Street, which follows the line of the now demolished east wall of the town is, of course, newer than the west side. It has, however, some buildings, remnants of buildings and features which deserve attention. Tynte's Castle is a much-altered, somewhat dilapidated late fifteenth- or sixteenth-century tower-house, of a kind very common in Ireland. It belonged to William Walshe, a prominent Youghal burgher and merchant, and, apparently, a confidant of the earl of Desmond. His fortunes crashed with those of the earl and he incurred forfeiture after the suppression of the earl's rebellion. In 1584, the tower-house was given to Sir Robert Tynte, who came to Youghal from Somerset, and whose wife, Elizabeth, was the widow of Edmund Spenser. Like the Benedictine priory, the building appears to be used as a workshop or store. This function is totally at variance with its historical and architectural importance.

Number 132, O'Neill Crowley Street, situated at the corner of that street and North Main Street, is interesting in that what appears to be a fifteenth- or early sixteenth-century stone doorway of Gothic style was set in the gable of the modern building. Meat Shambles Lane, which leads from North Main Street to the area of the port, was, no doubt, the part of the medieval and early modern town in which the butchering trade was established.

To the north of the town lie the ruins of the Dominican friary, erroneously described as an 'abbey'. This friary, dedicated to the Invocation of the Holy Cross and later to Our Lady of Thanks, was founded in 1268 by Thomas fitz Maurice fitz Gerald, who was buried here in 1298. Provincial chapters of the Dominican order were held here. The friary was suppressed during the Henrician reformation in Ireland but, thanks to the protection given to it by the earl of Desmond, it continued to function. Notionally, it was in the hands of William Walshe, to whom reference was made earlier, and to whom a lease was granted in 1543 and renewed in 1550. In 1548, Maurice, brother of the earl of Desmond, was custodian and William Walshe was responsible for the rent. Only after the fall of the earldom of Desmond in 1583 was the friary finally suppressed. By 1587, it had come into the hands of Sir Walter Raleigh and the buildings were destroyed.

In the late seventeenth century, there appear to have been a few dwellings north of the town beside the old highway to Cork. South of the walled town, according to Orme, detached one- and two-storeyed houses lined the road to the Franciscan friary which later developed into Friar Street. Nothing now remains of this friary which was the first Franciscan house in Ireland and which was founded in 1224 by Maurice fitz Gerald, the founder of the town of Youghal. The building was completed by Maurice's second son Thomas, who was also interred there. In all, seven earls of Desmond and many other Geraldines are said to have been buried in the church of this Franciscan friary. Provincial chapters of the Franciscan order were held here in 1300 and 1313. Under the protection of the earl of Desmond, the friars remained until 1583, when they were driven out or killed by English Protestants who destroyed everything and the place was abandoned.

The history of St Mary's church, the college of Youghal and the Dominican and Franciscan friaries further illustrates the importance of the earls of Desmond in the early history of Youghal. In the seventeenth century, however, Richard Boyle and his sons also played a formative role in the history of the town as a limb of English colonial administration in Ireland. Not only did he establish a free school, devoted to the promotion of Anglicanism and English culture, but also he did much to promote the town's economy. Youghal's exports increased in the course of the seventeenth century and it became the centre of the Irish wool export trade.

So prosperous and important was its port that, in the eighteenth century, many new public buildings were built, especially on the slob land to the east. These included the Tholsel which was built in 1753. New quays and docks were built, notably Salter's Quay (1716), Mannix Quay (1737), Green's Quay, and Nealon's Quay (1782) on which the new fish market was erected in 1811. In the eighteenth century the principal commodities exported were wheat, barley and oats, reflecting the massive growth in Irish tillage farming.

By the nineteenth century the town had expanded considerably further south and south-west and the railway arrived. In effect, these developments brought about the creation of a new town on the Cork side, one which, it has been said, 'has none of the picturesqueness of the old Youghal', but which developed 'as a seaside resort and pleasure centre famed for the excellence and safety of sea-bathing afforded by its miles of fine sands'.

However, the early twentieth century saw the collapse of Youghal as a seaport and a significant decline in its fishing industry. Little of that industry now remains. In the 1960s and 1970s, the policy of attracting foreign industry to Youghal had some notable successes, but this policy is now in jeopardy, not least because of recent international developments. These developments mark a new point of departure in the history of Youghal. The problems which the new conditions present will have to be addressed as a matter of urgency by the citizens of Youghal and, indeed, by us all.

Select bibliography
H. Wain: *The History of Youghal*, Cork, 1965
A. R. Orme: 'Youghal, County Cork – growth, decay, resurgence', *Irish Geography*, v (1966), pp. 121-49
A. F. O'Brien: 'The settlement of Imokilly and the formation and descent of the manor of Inchiquin', *Journal of the Cork Historical and Archaeological Society*, lxxxvii (1982), pp. 21-6
A. F. O'Brien: 'Medieval Youghal: the development of an Irish seaport trading town', *Peritia*, v (1986), pp. 346-78
A. F. O'Brien: 'The royal boroughs, the seaport towns and royal revenue in medieval Ireland', *Journal of the Royal Society of Antiquaries of Ireland*, cxviii (1988), pp.13-26
A. F. O'Brien: 'Politics, economy and society: the development of Cork and the Irish south-coast region *c.* 1170 to *c.* 1583', in P. O'Flanagan and C. G. Buttimer (eds), *Cork: History and Society: Interdisciplinary Essays on the History of an Irish County*, Dublin, 1993, pp. 83-154

WEXFORD

Kevin Whelan

TRYING to understand the creative process, Patrick Kavanagh once observed: 'On the stem of memory, imagination blossoms.' Our towns potentially provide many stems, many blossoms, especially if we envisage them as cumulative creations, embodying the collective biography of their past inhabitants, statements in stone which are at once accessible and democratic. Our streets and houses reflect the sedimentation of human experience through the streams of time. To use the language of postmodernism, exploration of our towns allows for micro-narratives not meta-narrative, a series of small stories truthful to the ceaseless fluidity of life as it is lived.

Looked at in this way, our towns retain the intimate, diverse histories of past generations; how they lived and worked, played and prayed, cursed and caroused in one small place which, itself, remained fixed in place as it changed through time, accumulating history organically, like a tree accumulating tree rings. Exploring a town's history then, is like stripping off the contemporary surface bark; looking at layer after superimposed layer, we seek to reveal the hidden interiors of the town's past. Taking Wexford as our example, let us see if we can make imagination blossom on the stems of its urban memories.

The town has a charm all of its own. Wexford is at once compact and cosmopolitan, a place where the tangible European whiff in the air is grounded by the solid, homely, lived-in streets. This Janus-headed interplay between the local and the exotic is appropriate to a town which for centuries has acted as a gateway to Ireland from Britain and the continent. Celt, Viking, Norman, Fleming, Dutch and English have all passed through here and the town retains their diverse imprints in its layout.

The earliest visible layer is now pinpointed by the spiky profile of Selskar Abbey, which is located on the site of an

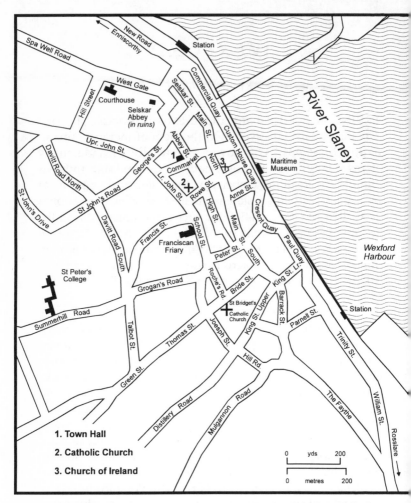

1. Town Hall
2. Catholic Church
3. Church of Ireland

Wexford, based on Ordnance Survey Road Atlas of Ireland, 1985

Early Christian monastery, of fifth- to eighth-century date. Billy Colfer has recently pointed out that the typically concentric shape of the monastic site can still be traced in the modern street plan. The monastery was located where the land-based route down the west bank of the Slaney met the estuary as it shallowed, which was a suitable site for a ferry across to the Castlebridge side – immemorially called 'Over-the-water' by generations of Wexford town folk.

In the ninth century, the Viking fleets nosing around the Irish coastline and sniffing up the estuaries inevitably found this site and appropriated it as their own. They rechristened the rock above the ferry point Selskar – seal rock – and they gave the town they founded alongside it the name Weisfjord, the harbour of the mud flats. Never was a name more appropriate. At times, the still mirror of the vast harbour surface can contrive to give the appearance of a Venetian lido, a scene from a Canaletto painting. But the mirror is deceptive, concealing the treacherous shallowness of the sprawling Slaney estuary. The Vikings presumably liked the security provided by the mud-clotted waters, whose channels needed to be intimately known to be safely negotiated. Otherwise, the oozing, cloying mud could seductively drag a ship into its soggy embrace, leaving it high and dry as the tide receded, exposing the famous Wexford sloblands – treacly expanses of glistening, dangerous mud.

The Vikings, consummate seamen whose ships drew only a shallow draught, felt comfortable here. As at Dublin and Waterford, the Viking town was located near a tributary stream entering the main river; a deep pool existed near its mouth, on the site of what is now the Crescent Quay, with its statue of Commodore John Barry. The stream's presence is recalled by the names of Stone Bridge and Paul Quay – a corruption of the west country English word, pill, meaning a tidal inlet. By 892, Wexford was one of the five principal Viking towns and part of their great network of trading ports which snaked down from their Scandinavian homeland along the ragged Atlantic coastline and round into the safe Mediterranean. Ireland was ideally placed to act as a halfway house for Viking European trade and Wexford was one of their nodes.

Like their other urban settlements, Viking Wexford was a narrow crescent on a slight ridge overlooking the waterfront. An earthen bank and ditch, like that of Wood Quay in Dublin, enclosed an urban area of about 10 hectares (25 acres). The Viking presence is now recalled in St Olaf's parish, and in Keyser's Lane, the 'road to the quay' of their town. The current Cornmarket is likely to have been their

Wexford in 1820 by Captain H. Mitchell, engraved by Short and Sutherland

market place, located just outside their town wall; indeed, it may even be the old monastic market, placed as it is in the standard location – south-east of the Selskar entrance.

Recent excavations at Bride Street have revealed very well-preserved Viking house remains, of characteristic timber and wattle construction, and with stylistic features known as Hiberno-Norse. Over the three centuries following the Viking foundation, considerable fusion with Gaelic culture had occurred. That assimilative process was rudely shattered in 1169 when the first small band of Norman warriors landed in south Wexford, at the behest of the Uí Chinnselaig king, Diarmait Uí Murchadha – subsequently known to Irish history as Diarmait na Gall – Dermot of the foreigners. Led by Robert Fitzstephen, the Normans immediately attacked Wexford – an indication of the town's strategic and economic importance. During the attack, they burned ships in the harbour, an event commemorated in the town's coat of arms, showing three burning ships and the motto 'per aquam et ignem' – 'through water and fire'.

Having captured the town, the Normans quickly set about establishing their own distinctive urban tradition. By the early thirteenth century, they had begun construction of an extensive town wall with mural towers, running along the line of the existing Viking rampart but extending to take in the market place, the ferry landing and the Selskar area. The north-south distinction in the town, which continues right up to the present day, may have originated in this expansion. To the south, a suburb grew up in the Faythe area. The evocative word 'Faythe' comes from the Gaelic word *fáiche*, a green, suggesting that an extra-mural fair site may have existed here. The Norman town as defined by its walls was about 25 hectares (more than 60 acres) in size – two and a half times that of the Viking town. Six gates – Castle, Bride, Peter, Keyser, John and West – punctuated the wall, as did a series of mural towers. Unlike in many other Norman towns, the wall did not run along the waterfront, which encompassed a series of individual wharves, accessed by lanes or slips, running along the sides of the long, narrow burgess strips which ran back from the main street towards the water. The wall cleverly followed the break of slope above the town; it was frequently refurbished but always on the same site. An excellent restoration of part of it can be seen at Westgate, complete with roof-walk and mural tower.

Typically, the Normans also built a large castle on a commanding site just outside the wall on the south end of the town. Demolished in the early eighteenth century, the site was occupied by a military barracks. It may still embody an earlier earthen motte fortification. Its memory is retained in the name Castle Hill Street. Like Kilkenny, therefore, the Anglo-Norman town of Wexford stretched between a Gaelic monastic site to the north and a castle to the south.

While the Normans were outstanding military and strategic thinkers, they were also skilled administrators, traders and churchmen. They used no less than twelve church sites in the town, and introduced the Franciscan order in 1268.

Characteristically, their friary was located just outside the town walls. By the mid-thirteenth century, there were about 365 burgage strips in the town, which suggests a peak medieval population of about 2,000. These narrow burgage strips can still be identified in the John Street and Faythe areas. Internally, the Norman town replicated the Viking pattern. Their main street continued to curve sinuously along the spine of the town, while a series of narrow foot lanes (like Oyster Lane and Keyser's Lane) ran to the harbour from it. The main street was the principal economic artery of the town. Today, it still has a medieval feel; people can almost reach across and shake hands with each other from the upper storeys of houses on either side of it. Walking Wexford main street today, one is literally following in the footsteps of the Vikings and the Normans.

The medieval town also had a Back Street, characteristically running parallel and upslope to Main Street. It also had two principal suburbs. The John Street area was, and remained, the town's craftsmen's quarter, packed full with carpenters, masons, bootmakers, coopers, butchers, etc. This noisy, dirty, roisterous street had a life all of its own, where town met country and myriad encounters shaped an incisive wit. Butchers' shambles, saltworks and smelly tanpits were tolerated here – the foul rag and bone shops on the fringe of the town. The second suburb, the Faythe, was a densely packed huddle of small thatched cabins, inhabited by fishermen, sailors and net-makers. From the Vikings, a seafaring strain entered the Wexford bloodstream and for centuries, the Faythe was a noted nursery of seamen.

Thus, by the end of the medieval period, the enduring framework of the modern town had been put in place, encompassing Gaelic, Viking and Norman elements. But in 1537 we get our first hint of the problem which was increasingly to bedevil the town. The sovereign and commons of Wexford petitioned the crown about the decline of their market, caused by 'the bad entrance to the harbour'. But the port's prosperity revived dramatically in the sixteenth and early seventeenth centuries, when it shipped two new exports – herring and oak. Both were in sustained demand in the rapidly expanding European metropolitan centres, especially London, Amsterdam and Lisbon. By 1612, the herrings were so abundant off the Wexford coast that boats from Devonshire and Cornwall came there to fish. The town did a roaring trade, and its merchants grew rich. 'Red herring houses' (for salting herrings) sprang up everywhere at the back of the quay, with their cobbled fish yards for gutting and gilling the glut of fish. Simultaneously, there was a massive export trade in oak pipe staves, ship timbers, laths and baulks. However, this booming trade had an unintended side effect. Rapid deforestation in the upper Slaney valley caused vastly increased run-off, delivering more mud and silt to the river which ceaselessly deposited it in ever thickening mud flats in the estuary. In 1635, the traveller William Brereton commented bluntly that the town 'is much prejudiced and damnified by a most vile barred haven' caused by 'two narrow bands of sand [which] run along on both sides of the channel into the sea'. The problem of the silting-up harbour was exacerbated by the sudden disappearance of the fickle herring in the 1620s, and by the slackening timber trade as the best and most accessible woods were cut down. By the late 1630s, a palpable gloom hung over the town, a gloom deepened by the increasing political vulnerability of its Catholic merchants who dominated it economically and socially. This complex of reasons may help explain why Wexford town and its Catholic elite participated so enthusiastically in the confederate politics of the 1640s.

Because of its experienced cadre of mariners, sailors and sea captains, and its undoubted shipping capacity, Wexford became the headquarters of the confederate navy. As in Viking times, the town's tricky harbour once more became an asset in terms of naval strategy. A cosmopolitan privateering industry mushroomed in the harbour where what were, in effect, licensed pirate ships lay safely at bay until ready to launch their predatory raids. The bigger British navy ships could not cross the bar and pursue them into Wexford harbour. So active and successful were the privateers that Wexford became known across Europe in the 1640s as 'the Dunkirk of Ireland'. This legalised piracy brought countless rich prizes to the town's Catholic merchants who financed and fitted out the privateers. The common English perception of Wexford as a nest of rapacious pirates contributed to the unbridled punitive savagery of Cromwell's assault on it in 1649. In the words of one contemporary, Cromwell aimed 'to make them vomit up again their stolen riches'. Regurgitation or not, Wexford's maritime star was never to be so much in the international ascendant again.

Shattered by the Cromwellian upheaval, with a harbour slowly choking, deserted by the lucrative herring and with the timber industry having cut its own throat through over-rapid exploitation, Wexford seemed to be facing an uncertain eighteenth century. Salvation came from the rapidly increasing output from Slaney valley agriculture, notably a tillage boom which accelerated as the century proceeded. In particular, Wexford became the principal centre for malt production nationally, being the main supplier of the Dublin distilleries. Malthouses replaced the obsolete herring houses; back lanes and gardens filled up with ubiquitous granaries, warehouses, kilns and all the other paraphernalia of a thriving agri-business. By 1796, there were over 200 malthouses in the town, and almost 100 small ships were employed carrying the malt to Dublin. Alongside the malthouses, there were also breweries and distilleries. These sturdy buildings, in attractive local stone and red brick, backboned the town's economy. However, the eighteenth-century town lacked architectural set-pieces to match its economic performance. In 1788, the prominent barrister John Philpott Curran, on walking through Wexford, observed that 'he never beheld a more indifferent looking town in his life'. His local friend replied to his notoriously ugly colleague, 'Why then it is like yourself – it is much better than it looks!'

For one thing, the town was famous for being both cheap and hospitable. The thrifty, hard-working baronies of Forth and Bargy lay to the south and supplied its markets with an abundance of good food – oysters, wild fowl, salmon, poultry, beef, mutton, butter, bread – all of the finest, freshest quality. Not for nothing were the Wexford slobs famous for their wild fowlers – the celebrated Shelmaliers, 'with their long barrelled guns from the sea'.

The town, buoyed up on the tillage boom, almost doubled its population between the 1730s and 1790s, but it failed to breach the 10,000 figure which would have moved it up from being merely a county town into a competitor with Waterford for the leadership of the south-east region. Wexford remained in some ways firmly rooted in its past; as late as 1764, half its 1,300 houses were thatched, and bull baiting continued in the Bull Ring until the last quarter of the century. The town elite were eager to modernise: a theatre royal, assembly rooms, circulating libraries, even a balloon ascent all came to the town, and by 1792, it had no less than six peruke makers to attend to its big wigs. The most prosperous merchants moved to the villa belt around the town – an aureole of Georgian residences of great charm overlooking the Slaney and the estuary, with fashionable names like Prospect, Belmont, Bettyville, Sallyville, Riversfield, Rockfield and Belvidere.

The town itself, though, stayed resolutely medieval in plan and fabric, mainly because it was in multiple ownership. There was no omnipotent magnate to remodel Wexford in enlightenment style. The fragmented ownership pattern, therefore, had the effect of fossilising the essentially medieval framework, insulating it from the sweeping changes which transformed Dublin, Limerick and Cork at this time. Only one eighteenth-century street appeared – George's Street – where a fine array of Georgian houses hosted the county's gentry, like the Colcloughs, Harveys and Rowes, in the winter social season. Existing main-street houses were also given a Georgian facade and their upper storeys now often preserve elegant Queen Anne windows.

Undoubtedly though, malting, milling, brewing and distilling underpinned the town. By 1790, Wexford was described as 'industrious, rich and prosperous'. Malting and its associated shipping were the main wealth generators. In 1783, a charitable organisation was set up in the town, and the two leading occupations among its contributors were maltster and ship captain.

In a way, the town's prosperity led to its deep politicisation in the turbulent 1790s, when it split on conservative and liberal lines. Indeed, the most spectacular building project of the eighteenth century was essentially a flamboyant political gesture. In an effort to outflank the conservative axis led by the marquis of Ely, the town's liberals, led by Bagenal Beauchamp Harvey and Cornelius Grogan, sponsored the building of a huge timber bridge across the estuary. This massive project was implemented by the Boston builder, Lemuel Cox, in 1794-5. By contrast, Ely's fountain in the Bull Ring seemed very small beer. The underlying tensions were exacerbated by the resurgent Catholic middle class, increasingly wealthy and articulate. In the long hot summer of 1798, the victorious United Irishmen held the town for almost a month, and established there what one contemporary called 'an embryo republic'. A small directory was created, composed of the distinctive United Irishman merger of Protestant reformers and Catholic activists. Their very real achievement was to maintain order and discipline in the town during that turbulent period. Indeed, so good was the control that very little property was damaged during the rebellion, and the town quickly settled back into its commercial mode in the early nineteenth century.

One of the first jobs to be undertaken was to rationalise the town quays. A 1790 visitor had observed with horror: 'I never saw worse quays in any seaport town', and reiterated the town's continuing harbour nightmare: 'The entrance is dangerous as the sands move and shift with every wind, by which means it is impossible for mariners to know the direct channel.' As ships got bigger and drew a greater draught of water, Wexford's shallow waters seemed less and less inviting. Desperate efforts were made to push the harbour front out in a search for deeper water. However, much of this tended to be piecemeal and unco-ordinated, because each merchant had his own wharf, making the quay a jagged crenellation. In the early nineteenth century, it was decided to rationalise these into one very long composite quay, to accommodate the numerous sailing ships of the period. Because these were both small and slow, lots of them were required: about a hundred in the malting trade alone, with names like *Neptune, Venus, Good Interest, Two Friends, Dreadnought* and *Lovely Kitty*. Because they were sailing ships, dependent on wind, weather and tide, they spent a long time in port and, therefore, occupied a large quay space. In 1837 the port had 110 registered vessels, but with a very small average capacity of about 60 tons.

With the rationalisation of the quay and the move towards deeper water, the space behind became available for colonisation by the town. In Wexford, as in Youghal and Drogheda, this involved building shops, timber yards, grain stores, sheds and warehouses on the reclaimed ground. Thus, a new commercial and industrial strip was inserted between the main street and the quay. As we have seen, the old medieval main street ran along the ridge and there is, accordingly, a steep drop towards the quay. Nicholas Furlong has pointed out that this has had a curious effect on the urban geography of the town. From the Bull Ring to the Peter's Street junction with South Main Street, all the pubs are on the quay side of the street, which had the required steep drop to provide cellar facilities. These pubs were especially patronised by the 600 seamen associated with the town in 1837, creating a lively, raucous, maritime atmosphere.

But despite all the frenetic effort to salvage its harbour's reputation, much of Wexford's trade drifted inexorably to the deep-water ports of New Ross and especially Waterford. As ships got bigger and bigger, Wexford's problems, unlike its harbour, deepened. A final nail in the port's coffin was the arrival of the railway. The Redmond family were instrumental in attracting the railway. Merchants, bankers, property speculators, entrepreneurs and politicians, the Redmonds were also involved in massive reclamation schemes. With characteristic Victorian optimism, they always believed in a technological fix for the harbour problem. But, in bringing in the railway, they virtually killed overnight the coasting trade to Dublin. However, the town's grain trade was still impressive and the solid market in the Model County hinterland encouraged investment in farm machinery manufacturing. The most famous of these was Pierce's, founded in 1839; its success encouraged the foundation of the Star Ironworks. Both were export and employment successes as long as the horse remained at the centre of agricultural production.

Nonetheless, as the Irish economy slowed perceptibly in the 1830s and 1840s, the town had an introspective, unprepossessing appearance. The ever-caustic *Parliamentary Gazetteer* of 1845 was scathing.

> The town as a whole is an ill-paved, filthy, repulsive place, most of its thoroughfares orientally narrow, and multitudes of its houses squalid, disgusting and pestiferous. No large or second rate town of Ireland seemed to us so malodorous and generally disagreeable as Wexford, excepting Galway, the Irish town of Athlone and the English town of Limerick!

Alongside the quay, the railways and agricultural machinery works, the other rapid developer in the nineteenth-century town was the Catholic church. By a technicality, the thirteenth-century Franciscan friary survived the penal laws, as it was located outside the town wall and, therefore, outside the corporation's jurisdiction. It continued in use as the sole and much-loved place of worship until the mid-nineteenth century, when population increase put intolerable pressure on it. It was then decided to build the celebrated twin churches of Bride Street and Rowe Street. Allegedly made exact facsimiles to neutralise north-south rivalry in the town, their Gothic-revival spires dominate the Wexford skyline – a soaring statement of the new assertiveness of the Catholic church. Other Catholic institutional buildings were also added to the town fringes in the nineteenth century – a smatter of convents and, most notably, St Peter's College with its Pugin-designed chapel of 1840.

Like those of most other Irish towns, Wexford's population contracted and the town's fabric remained relatively static in the century after the famine. While the grain trade kept the port on a life-support system, the writing was on its harbour walls. The sisyphean struggle with the shifting sands was finally abandoned with the decision to build the new port at Rosslare Harbour in the first decade of the twentieth century. Wexford quay then faded into picturesque obsolescence. Almost the only striking addition to the townscape in this period was the wonderful statue of the pikeman by Oliver Shepard, erected in the Bull Ring to commemorate the 1798 rising. This is one of the few outstanding pieces of public sculpture in an Irish town.

By the 1940s and 1950s, the town seemed to have withdrawn into itself. Its claustrophobic medieval feeling on grey misty days impressed itself so deeply on the young John Banville growing up in the town that he was later able to use it for his vivid recreations of the sombre small-town life of Mitteleuropa associated with the subject of his novels *Kepler* and *Copernicus*.

Another literary product of the town, the playwright Billy Roche, catches the waiting-for-something-to-happen feel of the 1950s town in his *Wexford Trilogy*. Since then, the town has entered a rapid phase of growth but much of this was concentrated on its fringes, leaving the historic core intact to a remarkable degree.

On a busy day, when the pedestrianised main street is packed and vivacious, it requires only a little imagination to make the stem of memory blossom. Even the distinctive Wexford town accent is a product of centuries of linguistic interchange between Gaelic, Norse, Flemish, French and English. A similar pluralism is revealed in the array of family names lovingly displayed on shop-fronts. Nowhere can the town's character be savoured so well as during its opera festival, when the gaily decorated narrow streets once more ring with a plethora of accents and the Theatre Royal is thronged by aficionados enjoying the programme of little-known masterpieces. This ancient setting blossoms then, awash with vibrancy, a town sure of its place and secure in its identity.

Select bibliography

P. H. Hore: *History of the Town and County of Wexford*, 6 vols, London, 1900-11

N. Furlong: *Loc Garman and Wexford*, Wexford, 1980

P. Reck: *Wexford: A Municipal History*, Wexford, 1987

K. Whelan (ed.): *Wexford: History and Society*, Dublin, 1987

M. Kehoe: *Wexford Town: Its Streets and People*, Wexford, 1989

B. Colfer: 'Medieval Wexford', *Journal of the Wexford Historical Society*, xiii (1991), pp. 5-29

LIST OF CONTRIBUTORS

Professor J. H. Andrews   Chepstow, Gwent, Wales

John Bradley   Department of Archaeology,
                                     University College, Dublin

Michael Byrne   Offaly Historical and
                                     Archaeological Society,
                                     Tullamore, County Offaly

George Cunningham   Parkmore, Roscrea, County
                                     Tipperary

Professor Patrick Duffy   Department of Geography,
                                     St Patrick's College,
                                     Maynooth

Dr Raymond Gillespie   Department of History,
                                     St Patrick's College,
                                     Maynooth

Carol Gleeson   Heritage Centre,
                                     Carlingford, County Louth

Paul Gosling   Department of Archaeology,
                                     University College, Galway

Dr Arnold Horner   Department of Geography,
                                     University College, Dublin

Dr Desmond McCabe   Centre for Urban History,
                                     University of Leicester

Dr A. F. O'Brien   Department of History,
                                     University College, Cork

Dr Tadhg O'Keeffe

Department of Archaeology,
University College, Dublin

Dr Philip Robinson

Ulster Folk and Transport
Museum, Cultragh, Belfast

Professor Etienne Rynne

Department of Archaeology,
University College, Galway

Professor Anngret Simms

Department of Geography,
University College, Dublin

Dr Kevin Whelan

Royal Irish Academy,
Dublin

IRISH COUNTRY TOWNS

Edited by
Anngret Simms and J. H. Andrews

Country towns are an important aspect of Irish identity, blending place and time in a unique fashion. Their stories reflect the formative periods of town foundation in Ireland: from Gaelic monastic sites to Anglo-Norman colonial settlements to early modern plantation towns.

The story of each town is here given added interest by a town plan and an evocative black-and-white illustration, usually nineteenth-century. A map gives an overview of all the towns featured in the book and classifies them according to their mode of origin.

The collective history of these Irish towns reflects the complexity of Irish civilisation in a more colourful way than could any chronological history.

The towns included in this book are Kells, Downpatrick, Carrickfergus, Maynooth, Enniscorthy, Bandon, Lurgan, Ennistymon, Castlecomer, Bray, Athlone, Dungarvan and Mullingar.

IRISH CITIES

Edited by
Howard Clarke

To accompany a series of Thomas Davis lectures on RTE radio, this publication draws on the leading experts in history, archaeology and historical geography to examine in detail the development of Belfast, Cork, Derry, Galway, Kilkenny, Limerick, Waterford and Dublin.

Fifteen essays discuss the early and later periods of development of these cities. Contributors include Professor Louis Cullen, Dr Jacinta Prunty, Dr Avril Thomas, Professor Gearóid MacNiocaill and the editor, Dr Howard Clarke.